AWAY WITH WORDS

Young Writers' 16th Annual Poetry Competition

It is feeling and force of imagination that make us eloquent.

How can I not dream while writing? The blank page gives a right to dream.

YoungWriters

Young Voices
Edited by Heather Killingray
& Mark Richardson

 Young**Writers**

First published in Great Britain in 2007 by:
Young Writers
Remus House
Coltsfoot Drive
Peterborough
PE2 9JX
Telephone: 01733 890066
Website: www.youngwriters.co.uk

SB ISBN 978-1 84602 873 1

Foreword

This year, the Young Writers' *Away With Words* competition proudly presents a showcase of the best poetic talent selected from thousands of up-and-coming writers nationwide.

Young Writers was established in 1991 to promote the reading and writing of poetry within schools and to the young of today. Our books nurture and inspire confidence in the ability of young writers and provide a snapshot of poems written in schools and at home by budding poets of the future.

The thought, effort, imagination and hard work put into each poem impressed us all and the task of selecting poems was a difficult but nevertheless enjoyable experience.

We hope you are as pleased as we are with the final selection and that you and your family continue to be entertained with *Away With Words Young Voices* for many years to come.

Contents

Lewis Spargo (10)	16
Katie Webb (9)	16
Magalie Wansongi (9)	16

Becket Primary School, Weston-Super-Mare

Ellie May Robinson (10)	17
Benjamin Abraham (9)	17
Rebecca Couch (10)	18
Nanine Balchin (11)	18
Kryzten Dellow (11)	19
Billy Hawkins (10)	19
Zoe Lasson (10)	20
Mia Howell & Katie Davies (9)	20
Tyler-Paige Harvey & Hannah Spearing (9)	21
Ashleigh Richards (10)	22
Elsie Taylor (9)	22
Gemma Cross (10)	23
Ellie-May Hancock (9)	23
Charlie Gibbons (10)	23
Hannah Mereweather (10)	24
Ryan Pountney (10)	24
Joe Morteo (10)	25
Connor Crowhurst (10)	25
Dexter Barter (10) & Luke James (9)	26
Adam Griffin (9)	26
Jemma Winchester (9)	26
Georgina Morgan (10) & Charlotte Venn (9)	27

Earlham Primary School, Forest Gate

Ibrahim Rahman (8)	27
Ravinder Singh (8)	27
Sidiq Nadeem (8)	28
Sanjidah Yasmin Chowdhury (7)	28
Humza Rahman (9)	28
Danielle Foley (8)	29
Alfie Cook (8)	29
Samiha Begum	29
Fabbiha Rahat Islam (8)	30
Mikal Ana Lafronté (8)	30
S Mohammed Hussain Nagvi (7)	30
Aini Kamal (8)	31

Ferdos Mohammed Ahmed (9)	31
Mohamed Saiamul Alam Saiam (7)	31
Justina Kapociute (7)	32
Vitesh Dav (7)	32
Ameerah Rahman (7)	32
Manzurul Islam (9)	33
Mikal Vicente (7)	33

Forest School, Timperley

Aisha Latif (6)	33
Harry MacDonald (10)	34
Kimberley Johal (10)	34
Xouxhaenya Henry	35
James Campbell (10)	35
James Farrow (10)	36
Edward Ward (10)	36
Kelly Peters (10)	37
Katie Brayzier (10)	37
Georgina Nelson (10)	38
Daniel Waxman (11)	38
George Johnston (8)	39
Lauren Richards (10)	39
Olivia Prickett (11)	40
Connor Rutherford (7)	40
Amy Connell (7)	40
Alison Poon (10)	41
Edward Galley (7)	41
Rebecca Greaves (7)	42
Olivia Baldwin (7)	42
Abigail Turner (7)	42
Sana Naik (7)	43
Kieren Sharma (7)	43
Jack Fisher (7)	43
Giulia Baggaley Simpson (10)	44
Chetan Dusara (10)	44

Hazeldown Primary School, Teignmouth

Roslyn Harrion (8)	45
Anastasia Weston (8)	45
Mikey Evans (8)	46
Annie Salter (8)	46

Georgia McGrane (8)	46
Amy Broderick (8)	46
Jessica Morris (8)	47
Daniel Harvey (8)	47
Sophy Moyle (8)	48
Lurie Moore (8)	48
Emily Northcott (8)	48
Samuel Speed (9)	49
Jazmine White (9)	49
Matthew Brooks (8)	49
Will Kelly (8)	50
Tom Libby (8)	50
Matthew Shimell (8)	50
Holly Reed (8)	51
Sophie Rainbow (8)	51
Sam Peat (8)	51
Helena Cope (8)	52
Jack Phillips (8)	52
Jake Peat (8)	53
Christopher Johnson (8)	53
Jordan Pocock (8)	53
Callum Booker (8)	54
Alisha-Mae Aplin (8)	54
Adam Lee (8)	54
Erin Hodgson (8)	55
Ellen Bryan (8)	55
Leigh-Anne Preston (8)	55

Lipson Vale Primary School, Lipson

Luke Bishop (10)	56
Francesca Griffiths (10)	56
Rachel Miller (10)	57
Faye West (10)	57
Laura Farley (10)	57
Sam Bailey (11)	58
Jessica Mallory (10)	58
Elland Hawker (10)	59
Gemma Humphrey (10)	59
Michaella Toombs-Dunleavy (10)	60
Sam Carey (10)	60
Macauley Cole (10)	60

Erin Crisp (10)	61
Curtis Young (10)	62
Connie Jane Veale (10)	62
Maddy Luxton (10)	63
Hannah Wills (10)	63
Alexander Pethick (11)	64
Kate Sands (10)	64
Evelyn Francis (10)	65
Deanna Pealing (10)	65
Fern Buller (10)	65
Charlotte Goodchild (10)	66

Oaklands Primary School, Welwyn

Aimee Rayner-Okines (9)	66
Emily Lauran Stacey (8)	66
David Ackland (7)	67
George James Wallis-Smith (9)	67
Holly Swinburne (8)	67
Robert Drew (8)	68
Zara Hoy (8)	68
Will Vaughan (8)	68
Philippa Stephens (8)	69
Megan Jackson (7)	69
Niamh Whicher & Renée Beane (7)	69
Adam Webster (8)	70
Eleanor Smith (9)	70
James Firth (9)	70
Lucy Reynolds (9)	71
Maxwell Brendish (9)	71
Amanveer Benning (9)	71
Josh Genever (11)	72
Naomi Baycroft (7)	72
Delorice Murudzwa (8)	72
Samuel Borrie (10)	73
Elizabeth Spear (9)	73
Hannah Young (9)	73
Oliver Stephens (10)	74
Charlotte Birtles (9)	74
Richard Vaughan (10)	75
Sarah Cox (9)	75
Luke Fuller (10)	76

Harry Ironton (9)	76
Ryan O'Driscoll (10)	77
Harvey Turner (9)	77
Robert White (9)	78
Sulaimaan Mughal (9)	78
Hannah Kempster (10)	79
Samuel Curtis (9)	79
George Ironton (10)	80
Katie Deards (8)	80
Emily Beswick (10)	81
Nathan Donnelly (8)	81
Matthew Walton (9)	82
Laura Goodacre (8)	82
Robert Vaughan (10)	83
Ben Wilson (8)	83
Daniel Hughes (10)	84
Mark Wong (10)	84
Connor Wilson (10)	85
Shannee Rogers (10)	85
Geraden Wren (11)	86
Emily Tomlinson (9)	86
Georgina Shortland (10)	87
James Curtis (9)	87
Katie Genever (8)	88
Vishva Naik (9)	88
Jamie Kempster (8)	88
Rhian Mather (10)	89
Joshua Heyman (9)	89

Purley Oaks Primary School, Croydon

Mica Wilkins (8)	90
Haiden Noel (8)	90
Manisha Patel (10)	91
Dante Smith (8)	91
Samantha Collins (9)	91
Nathan Samuel (8)	92
Louise Covington (8)	92
Somer Wigger (8)	93
Mollie Bernadino (8)	93
Perrie Aungmya (8)	94
Brito Dos Reis (9)	94

Brandon Aung-Mya (10)   135
Kyra Lord-Lindsay (7)   136
Sherelle Greenidge-Ifill (7)   136
James Lockwood (7)   137
Tamikaine Trimblett (8)   137
Cira Fisher-Jaine (9)   138
Harvey Norman (8)   139
Yasmin Basith (7)   139
Daniel Allen (7)   140
Morgan Payne (8)   140

St John's CE (VA) Primary School, Clifton
Grace Victoria Perryman (8)   141
Robert Winslow (8)   141
Holly Tasker (8)   142
Leo Stross (8)   142
Charlotte Jones (8)   143
Bethany Tottles (8)   143
George Price Hulin (8)   143
James Owens (8)   144
Oliver Beaumont (7)   144
Adam Shaw (8)   145
Harry Wood (8)   145
Jake Guest (8)   146
Jack Ellis (8)   146
Alexandra Gledhill (8)   147
Anya Finch (8)   147
Daniel Newton (8)   148
Emily Rebecca Hirst (8)   148
Dominic Heyhoe (8)   149
Charlotte Anne Tankard (8)   149
Andrew Owen (8)   150
Callum Wilkie (8)   150
Siân Lewis (8)   151
Joshua Maskill (8)   151

Two Moors Primary School, Tiverton
Tiegan Hezzell (8)   152
Kayleigh Messenger (8)   152
Charlotte Chidgey (8)   153
Kayleigh Harris (8)   153

The Poems

A Poem Mixed

If I were king, I'd make $20+30=$fish
If I were king, I'd make kids' toys free
If I were king, I'd forbid school for a year
If I were king, I'd make new games be free and quick
It makes me laugh when my friends go crazy
And then they get lazy
If I were king, I'd make school end at 2pm
Up and away the plane goes,
Where it goes, nobody knows.

Jordan Small (9)
Ashburton Junior School, Croydon

Darkness

Darkness is black like the night sky
It sounds like the wind whistling in your ear
Darkness tastes like melting chocolate in your mouth
It smells like a burnt-out fire
Darkness looks like evil bats flapping their wings to fly into the forest
It feels like someone is following me on the streets at night
Darkness reminds me of blankness and you're gasping for air.

Aine Curran (9)
Ashburton Junior School, Croydon

Sadness

Sadness is pale blue like tears falling from my eyes
Sadness feels like not being able to talk to anyone
Sadness sounds like a drum inside me
Sadness tastes like stale water I'm drinking out of a grubby cup
Sadness looks like an empty room, with nothing in it but my tears.

Hania Wisskirchen (9)
Ashburton Junior School, Croydon

Happiness

Happiness is sweet yellow like vanilla ice cream
Happiness sounds like wonderful music, especially pop
Happiness tastes like a red lolly made out of sweets
Happiness smells of lovely roses flying in the air
Happiness looks like people smiling in Disneyland
Happiness feels really joyful, when people are playing a game
Happiness reminds me of good times
Like playing with my best friends.

Mantas Zukaitis (9)
Ashburton Junior School, Croydon

Happiness

Happiness is soft blue like the peaceful ocean
It sounds like the opening of a birthday present
Happiness is like licking a melting ice cream
It smells like a brand new day
Happiness looks like the sun setting
It feels as smooth as silk
Happiness reminds me of having a party with my family and friends.

Conah White (10)
Ashburton Junior School, Croydon

Silence

Silence is white like a pillow
It sounds like the classroom is empty
It tastes like pink candyfloss
It smells like smoke turning towards me
It looks like a large moon
It feels like the freezing cold wind, falling from the air.

James Thurston (9)
Ashburton Junior School, Croydon

Hunger

Hunger is grey like a dark, stormy cloud
Hunger sounds like people's tummies growling at you
Hunger tastes like pizza or chicken nuggets and lots of other food
Hunger smells like McDonald's, but there isn't any there
Hunger looks like an empty stomach
Hunger feels like when your tummy is rumbling
Hunger reminds me of when I'm hungry for dinner.

Amy Braud (9)
Ashburton Junior School, Croydon

Fear

Fear is dark blue like a sea
It sounds like a red and black slithering snake coming to get you
Fear tastes as bitter as lemon
It smells like an onion
Fear looks like a rainy, thundery day
It feels like a dinosaur chasing you away
It reminds me of death because it's disturbing thinking how they die.

Letwin Kangausaru (9)
Ashburton Junior School, Croydon

Fear

Fear is grey like gloomy clouds
Fear feels like an arrow through your heart
Fear looks like fire to your eyes
Fear sounds like rain drumming on your head
Fear smells like sea water up your nose.

Harvey Searle Vian-Smith (9)
Ashburton Junior School, Croydon

The Mad Professor

The mad professor has wild, sticky-up hair
He also has a pale, white face
His eyes are as black as night
And his fingerprints leave no trace
He likes to keep the children
So he can stuff his face.

Yes, so he can stuff his face
And he carries a great big sack
To put the heads of the children in
For his midnight snack.

Sophie Scamp (9)
Ashburton Junior School, Croydon

Happiness

Happiness is baby-blue like the sky
It sounds like hummingbirds humming
It tastes like a cup of sugar
It smells like I'm surround by wild flowers
It looks like I'm in the countryside
It feels like I'm in paradise.

Alisha Wisdom-Francis (9)
Ashburton Junior School, Croydon

Darkness

Darkness is as black as night
Darkness is like a volcano erupting
Darkness is like the taste of burnt toast
Darkness is like smelling rotten eggs
Darkness is like an empty cave in the year zero
Darkness is like reminding me of death.

Robert Jenkins (9)
Ashburton Junior School, Croydon

The Mad Professor

The really mad professor,
Was in a terrible mess,
He was always terribly busy
And was always under stress,
He tried so hard to be happy,
But he was happy less and less.

Yes, he was happy less and less,
He was really rather glum,
He didn't have a father,
He didn't have a mum.

The really mad professor,
Was in his library,
He never went ten minutes,
Without a cup of tea
And waved his arms quite wildly,
When he heard a buzzing bee.

When he heard a buzzing bee,
He remembered being stung,
He wasn't told what not to touch,
Cos he didn't have a mum.

The mad professor had a dog,
A potion he did make
And turned the dog into a frog
And baked him in a cake.

Laura Guild (9)
Ashburton Junior School, Croydon

Silence

Silence is white like a fluffy cloud
It's like a school room at the end of the day
It tastes like candyfloss melting in your mouth
It feels like you can work perfectly
It reminds me of deaf people.

Safa Akboudj (10)
Ashburton Junior School, Croydon

Love

Love is when I get cuddles
Love is pink
Love is when you get a new toy
Love is when you care for someone
Love is when you get sweets
Love is when you get a baby brother or sister
Love is my parents.

Emmy Hearne (9)
Ashburton Junior School, Croydon

Darkness

Darkness is black like being locked in a closet
Darkness sounds like your heart beating
Darkness is like tasting a Mars bar
Darkness looks like the end of the world
Darkness feels like someone is going to get you
Darkness reminds me of the power cutting out.

Ben Roddy (9)
Ashburton Junior School, Croydon

Love

Love is white like the fluffy clouds
Love sounds like wind swishing in the air
It tastes like water washing in your mouth
It smells like sweet sugar
Love looks like melted chocolate
Love feels like soft, cuddly teddies.

Thomas Davies (9)
Ashburton Junior School, Croydon

Hate

Hate is black like nothingness
It sounds like thunder booming in my head
Hate tastes like acid inside my stomach
Hate smells like smoke polluting the air
It looks like fire keeping others away from me
It feels like a vibrating shake destroying everything in sight
Hate reminds me of pain and sadness.

Ethan Scarse (9)
Ashburton Junior School, Croydon

Anger

Anger is red like a fierce roaring fire
Anger sounds like a bomb exploding
Anger tastes like acid
Anger smells like burning smoke
Anger looks like red flames in my eyes
Anger feels like a bullet through your heart
Anger reminds me of hurting someone.

Hanif Charles-Berry (9)
Ashburton Junior School, Croydon

Happiness

Happiness is a bright orange colour, like the sunset
It sounds like birds singing beautifully and nicely
Happiness tastes like pink candyfloss
It smells like lavender perfume
Happiness looks like someone full of joy.

Helen Mireku (9)
Ashburton Junior School, Croydon

Detention

Have you ever wondered,
Where kids go when they have detention?
Well, I can answer that,
You see, all teachers are witches
And they try to gobble you up!
First they suck your blood,
Then they pop out your eyes
And make them into pies,
For the next staff meeting.
Next they start eating the gooey stuff inside,
I haven't done that in class yet,
So I don't know what that gooey stuff is called.
Then they stitch you up and fill you
With the want to be a teacher's pet.
So, if someone asks you, if you
Would like to help in detention say, 'I'll pass.'
But if you creep upon a teacher and pull off their wig
You will find that Miss Bella is a fella!
But if you think that's bad,
You should see the teaching assistants!

Alice Glasgow (10)
Ashburton Junior School, Croydon

Fun

Fun is colourful like a rainbow
Fun sounds like laughing your heart out
Fun smells like freshly baked doughnuts
Fun looks like you're having a good time
Fun feels like a tickly hand
Fun reminds you of playing with your friends.

Jordan Cox (9)
Ashburton Junior School, Croydon

If I Had Wishes . . .

If I had wishes . . .
I would wish to fly
So that I could glide by

If I had wishes . . .
I would wish not to be seen
So that no one would know where I had been

If I had wishes . . .
I would wish for a cute little pup
And it would keep bounding up

If I had wishes . . .
I would wish for my dreamy world to come alive
So that I could do my beaver jive

If I had wishes . . .
I would wish for the skill to walk on water
So that I wouldn't have to be a porter

If I had wishes . . .
I would wish to finally stop writing this
So that I wouldn't have another wish!

Nicola Compton (9)
Ashburton Junior School, Croydon

Darkness

Darkness is as black as the mud on your football
It sounds like a rocket launching
It tastes like burnt chicken crunching in your mouth
It smells like the sewers
It is a black hole in space
It reminds me of a black cat.

Matthew George (9)
Ashburton Junior School, Croydon

When I Grow Up, I Would Like To Be . . .

When I grow up, I would like to be . . .
Rich and famous on TV.
When I grow up, I would like to be . . .
Called your Royal Majesty.

When I grow up, I would like to be . . .
In a house, with a wife.
When I grow up, I would like to be . . .
A happy man, with a lovely life.

When I grow up, I would like to be . . .
The world's strongest man.
When I grow up, I would like to be . . .
A scientist with the world's biggest fans.

Christopher Scamp (9)
Ashburton Junior School, Croydon

When I Grow Up

When I grow up, I would like to be a star
And drive a big, flashy car.

When I grow up, I would love to sing
With my bling-bling.

When I grow up, I would like to play
With my fluffy ball.

When I grow up, I would like to be a teacher
Because I like telling people off.

When I grow up, I would like to be
A football player.

Kadeja Clarke (10)
Ashburton Junior School, Croydon

An Alien Invasion

Aha!
It's just been,
Announced on the TV,
That aliens have been seen!
Run away, run away, as far as you can,
Be scared, panic, yes, even you, the Queen!
The aliens have been sighted,
You shouldn't be excited,
Because aliens have been seen!

They're scary, green and ugly,
They have eight eyeballs,
The aliens are slimy, as well as strong,
You wouldn't want to go wrong
'Cause they're as hard as brick walls,
Now help! Fight! Don't be fools!
They're shooting fireballs!

Jonathan Bare (9)
Ashburton Junior School, Croydon

Sweet Roses

Red is for roses
People sniffing around the roses
Roses are beautiful, just like me
The trees like roses
You can look and see.

The sky is blue
And violets are blue
Children are running around
Stamping on the ground.

My friends wear pink
My friends wear blue
My friends are funny
Like me and you!

Rachael King (9)
Ashburton Junior School, Croydon

How Mad?

How mad?
When you
Drop your chocolate ice cream.

How mad?
When your chocolate melts
In your pocket.

How mad?
When you drop
Your Haribo.

How mad?
When you drop
Your bike.

How mad?
When you run
Into a lamp post.

How mad?
When you pass wind
And everyone looks at you!

Reece Carosielli (9)
Ashburton Junior School, Croydon

I Will Soar

Up and away, I soar in the sky,
I soar smoothly, with birds passing by.
Up and away, birds fly every day,
They fly in a very funny way.
Up and away, I will soar,
Looking down at the floor.
Up and away, balloons float,
Even over the sea, from a boat.

Megan Martin (10)
Ashburton Junior School, Croydon

How Happy?

How happy?
When you play
On a lovely green
Football pitch
With John Terry.

How happy?
When you find
A stick of bubblegum
In your pocket.

How happy?
When you discover
You can swim
Like a dolphin.

How happy?
When you find
A six-legged spider.

How happy?
When you trim
The long green grass
Lots of creatures.

Steven Snowling (9)
Ashburton Junior School, Croydon

Rules

Rules, rules, stinking rules
You have to follow
All the rules
Make one mistake
You have to stay in
Your resting break.

Girre Girre (10)
Ashburton Junior School, Croydon

Darkness

Darkness is as pitch-black as a tunnel creeping out of the daylight
It sounds like silence beating at my brain
It tastes as dry as fear
Darkness smells like the fresh air tickling my nostrils
It looks like nothing at all
Darkness feels scary like you're going down
                              a super-fast roller coaster
It reminds me of sleeping in the night.

Amber Whitlock (9)
Ashburton Junior School, Croydon

Anger

Anger is as red as a fiery furnace
Anger sounds like thunder and lightning
Anger tastes as sour as a lemon
Anger smells as bad as sulphur
Anger looks like the middle of a volcano
Anger feels like molten lava
Anger reminds me of burning wood.

Daniel Spargo-Mabbs (9)
Ashburton Junior School, Croydon

If I Were King

If I were king, I would make $11 \times 30 \div 10 \times 0 = 1$
If I were king, I would try to take over France
If I were king, I would make there be no homework in Britain
If I were king, I would make eggs turn into chocolate
If I were king, I would forbid child abuse
If I were king, the world would be made of candy.

Jack Richards (10)
Ashburton Junior School, Croydon

I'm A Lean, Green Wrestling Machine

I'm a lean, green wrestling machine
Everyone glances at me
I'm lean and green
Sometimes mean
I can be good, but also can be bad.

If you see someone
Who is a wrestling machine
You know they will be mean.

Stefanie Toomey-Jenkins (10)
Ashburton Junior School, Croydon

The Moon

The moon is a shimmering yo-yo,
That is tossed across the sky,
Changing once in a while,
In a bed of shiny stars and deep blackness,
Sleeping softly,
Making a quiet *'zzzz'!*

Kate Shillabeer (9)
Ashburton Junior School, Croydon

Love

Love is red like your heart and lips
Love sounds like your heart beating
Love tastes like melted chocolate
Love smells like sweet strawberries
Love feels like soft silk
Love reminds me of happy times.

Chanté Thomas (9)
Ashburton Junior School, Croydon

The Mad Professor's Daughter Continued . . .

So, now we're writing a letter
And it started with a dear
Please can you get us out
Tom has got a tear
We're all stuck in the dungeon
Shivering with fear.

Yes, shivering with fear
They do not give us water
Locked up in a cage
By the mad professor's daughter.

Lewis Spargo (10)
Ashburton Junior School, Croydon

The Moon

The moon is a shiny ball of cheese
Falling across the sky
Spinning on its axis
Losing pieces along its way
Glowing and glittering
Soaring and swaying
Across space.

Katie Webb (9)
Ashburton Junior School, Croydon

The Moon

The moon is a shimmering tennis ball
That is spinning round and round like a cartwheel
Coming and hiding from the Earth
Giving good dreams to children
With glittering long arms for care.

Magalie Wansongi (9)
Ashburton Junior School, Croydon

Touching The Void

Above me, the sun is a gleaming ball of wonder
Melting the ice as far as I can see.

I don't know how to go on
I feel hurt, abandoned
I feel our friendship is broken.

Below me, the ice-cold, shimmering snow
Is a white suffocating blanket
Covering the rocky landscape.

I'm scared, hopeless and lonely.

Around me is sparkling snow
Like a shower of clear ice crystals
Covering all the caves.

I can hear a voice shouting death
It is beating and beating
In my head
The rope was cut
Is life almost over?

Ellie May Robinson (10)
Becket Primary School, Weston-Super-Mare

My Brother

He's a playful brother every day,
He's as great as New York city and that is really great,
He's as comfy as a sofa, squishy and soft,
He's a midday brother,
He's a ferocious shark rushing his way through the deep blue sea,
He's a constantly yapping dog all day and all night,
A jumping, snarling kangaroo,
Strong and determined body builder,
A falcon flying to the sun,
A strong kicker.

Benjamin Abraham (9)
Becket Primary School, Weston-Super-Mare

Touching The Void

Below, an endless drop
Life hanging on by a rope.

I am trapped,
Cold
Alone
In a frozen prison.

Thoughts of death twirling round my mind.

Wind as an endless torture
Following a lifeless friend below.

Sun beating down, but time seems to have stopped
As the snow does not melt.

At the beginning, I thought we would make it -
Now, hope seems gone.

Rebecca Couch (10)
Becket Primary School, Weston-Super-Mare

Touching The Void

Sun shining
A frozen meteorite
Clouds hover over the mountain
Like swans flapping beautiful, feathery wings.

Pain, leg broken, can't walk!

Isolated, hopeless,
Alone in an abandoned white landscape.

The rope is cut
I'm left for dead
Falling
Life whizzing past me.

I call twice
No one is there.

Nanine Balchin (11)
Becket Primary School, Weston-Super-Mare

Touching The Void

Joe - a good friend,
Thought he was dead,
Guilt, my fault he had fallen?

Terrified,
Cut the rope,
Tears turned into icicles,
As they dropped down my frozen face.

Golden sun,
An eternal ball
Of glowing fire,
Around me, icy wind,
Shivering,
I knew I had betrayed my best friend.

Kryzten Dellow (11)
Becket Primary School, Weston-Super-Mare

Touching The Void

Above me I see no hope
I can't get out of this frozen fortress
I can't get out of this icy jaw
Death is coming to take me to my cold coffin
I'm alone, deserted and numb
You left me for dead
I have lost all hope
Get me out
I need help!
When I fell, I knew you cut my lifeline
I know I'm alone
Life is almost lost.

Billy Hawkins (10)
Becket Primary School, Weston-Super-Mare

Touching The Void

Above me is a man holding a strong rope
I am near to death
Below me are ice-like crystals
I am near to death
A man has just cut the rope
I am near to death
I have frostbite
I am near to death
I call his name
He does not listen
I am near to death
I have a broken leg
I am near to death!

Zoe Lasson (10)
Becket Primary School, Weston-Super-Mare

Autumn Times

Cooler weather,
In autumn time,
Having a little breeze,
Down the seaside.

Conkers flying here and there,
Like prickly balls,
Will you win,
Or will you lose?

Acorns dropping,
From way up high,
It felt like they were coming from the sky.

Mia Howell & Katie Davies (9)
Becket Primary School, Weston-Super-Mare

The Best Autumn Ever

I remember
When the shiny conkers
Fell out of their shells
Like a bouncy ball.

I remember
When the baby acorns
Tumbled out of their bouncy cups.

I remember
When the leaves
Turned to fire
As a fireball.

I remember
When the bombs dropped
From the trees.

I remember
When the beans
Fell out of a huge pod.

I remember
When the apples
Fell out of the burning tree.

I remember
When the pointed fingers
Fell out of the human tree.

I remember
The conkers rolled over
The crunchy leaves.

I remember
When the leaves blew in the wind
Like a feather.

I remember
When pink petals fell off
The pretty tree.

Tyler-Paige Harvey & Hannah Spearing (9)
Becket Primary School, Weston-Super-Mare

Touching The Void

Above me, the sun is like a golden eye
In the high blue sky.

I feel scared, hurt and alone.

Below me, is icy cold, shimmering snow
A white suffocating blanket
Covering the vast mountain
I feel trapped, in a prison
And I feel like I am going to die
Our friendship is almost gone.

All around me, is a thick, freezing layer of mist
I know you might have thought I was dead

But I called you twice and no answer
I am helpless and abandoned.

Ashleigh Richards (10)
Becket Primary School, Weston-Super-Mare

My Brother

He's a bouncy chair,
He's a bolt of lightning,
An electric shock,
A fizzy drink,
He's my Jim-Bob.

He's Bugs Bunny,
A ripe tomato,
A tiger ready to pounce,
He's my tornado.

The brightest light in the solar system,
The sound of a howler monkey ready to kill
He's my candy world ready to be eaten.

Elsie Taylor (9)
Becket Primary School, Weston-Super-Mare

Touching The Void

Shivering nervously in front of the massive mountain
Crystal clear air
Will I make it?
Determined to finish
Shaking, I take the rope
I conquer my nerves
I climb nearer to the misty sky
Fiery sun cannot melt the rocky white ice
Half frozen - halfway
My loyal, trusting friend slipped.

Gemma Cross (10)
Becket Primary School, Weston-Super-Mare

My Friend

She's a soft, leather chair,
She's a cute rabbit bouncing high,
She's a tidy bedroom,
She's a Kelly Clarkson CD,
She's a sunny summer morning,
She's a golden bird singing.

Ellie-May Hancock (9)
Becket Primary School, Weston-Super-Mare

My Mentor

She is a comfy, wonderful beanbag,
She's a sparkling goldfish,
A peaceful desert land,
She's soft rain gently tapping on a windowpane,
A bright, glowing, setting sun.

Charlie Gibbons (10)
Becket Primary School, Weston-Super-Mare

Touching The Void

Above me snow falls onto my face
Like crystals
So cold I can't move my mouth.

I am freezing, helpless
I can't move my arms.

Below me is ice glittering like sharp diamonds
I don't want to fall, because I know I will die.

I have lost my trust with my best friend
I don't know why he cut the rope
I feel like he deserves to die too.

All around me, lots and lots of snow
I can't touch it, because it's too cold.

I am at the edge of my life
So scared that I might die.

Hannah Mereweather (10)
Becket Primary School, Weston-Super-Mare

Touching The Void

Above me, the golden sun
Staring at me like a great god.

I feel terrified, lost, alone.

Below, three hundred feet down,
An icy grave waits for me.

I'm hanging only by my waist,
I'm petrified, frozen, lost.

I take my last glance around me
Before my life is demolished.

I have no hope.

My fate is sealed.

Ryan Pountney (10)
Becket Primary School, Weston-Super-Mare

Touching The Void

Above me, the sun was like a golden eye
In the dark blue sky
I was demolished and lost
And full of pain
Hanging on to the rope I saw

Rocks tumbling down from the mighty mountain
Like an eruption.

All around me, snow
Is like a shower
Of clear ice crystals
Surrounding the cave.

I felt abandoned.

He cut the rope on our friendship.

Joe Morteo (10)
Becket Primary School, Weston-Super-Mare

Touching The Void

When I fell, I felt deserted
Abandoned, hope had gone for me.

Above me, the steaming hot sun
Like a giant ball of wonder
Melting the ice as far as I can see.

Below me is a snowy grave
Just waiting for me
To fall into its trap.

I feel death about to approach me.

Connor Crowhurst (10)
Becket Primary School, Weston-Super-Mare

Reflections Of Autumn

Fire leaves falling from the glowing tree
Flaming acorns on the tree or falling like red balls.

Conkers carrying suitcases in the autumn
Conkers like hedgehogs falling from the sky.

As red and round as a red ball
As shiny as a light glowing in the dark.

Long green chicken legs
As thin as a pencil on a piece of paper.

Dexter Barter (10) & Luke James (9)
Becket Primary School, Weston-Super-Mare

My Brother

He's a puffa on fire,
He's in the land of PS2,
He's a four o'clock person,
He's a lazy dog,
He's the sound of evil,
The colour of blue,
A bird going to its doom,
A goofy-voiced person.

Adam Griffin (9)
Becket Primary School, Weston-Super-Mare

My Friend

She's a bouncy chair,
A purring cat,
She's a golden palace,
The sound of happiness,
She's the sunny morning of spring.

Jemma Winchester (9)
Becket Primary School, Weston-Super-Mare

Changes That Take Place In Autumn

The leaves are changing colour,
From as green as grass,
To as brown as chocolate.

The hot smell of blackberries,
In a blackberry pie.

The leaves falling to the ground,
To make the carpet of colours.

The red-hot ball of fire,
Shining upon the icy, glass water.

The hedgehogs tumbling across,
In the cold, breezy night.

Georgina Morgan (10) & Charlotte Venn (9)
Becket Primary School, Weston-Super-Mare

Scary And Spooky

The colour of scary and spooky is black like the night
The taste of scary and spooky is chilli
The smell of scary and spooky is blood
The feeling of scary and spooky is like touching a monster
When it is scary and spooky, I hear scary and spooky growling
This reminds me of a knight.

Ibrahim Rahman (8)
Earlham Primary School, Forest Gate

Anger

Anger sounds like a blistering drum like your heart beating fast
Anger tastes like the hottest chilli on Earth
Anger smells like the worst shoe that smells of a bad odour
Anger looks like a type of slime
Anger feels like lava burning your hands.

Ravinder Singh (8)
Earlham Primary School, Forest Gate

Greediness

The colour is multicoloured,
With hundreds of colours mixed
It tastes like millions of foods,
Like burgers, fish and chips and even chicken and chips
All of it in my mouth,
All spicy and tasty
It smells like a chicken burger and some chips
It looks like a multicoloured flower
And feels like lots of food in your mouth
With everyone starving
And it reminds me of a giant chocolate!

Sidiq Nadeem (8)
Earlham Primary School, Forest Gate

Anger

Anger is red like a glaring sun
It sounds like a loud thunderstorm
It feels hot like a volcano
It smells like a burning fire
It tastes like burnt toast
It reminds me of the day of punishment.

Sanjidah Yasmin Chowdhury (7)
Earlham Primary School, Forest Gate

Anger

It sounds like a volcano erupting
It tastes like sour lemons
It smells like burning toast
It looks grey like smoke
I can feel my mouth burning
It reminds me of violence.

Humza Rahman (9)
Earlham Primary School, Forest Gate

Anger

Anger is the colour of red
Like someone hating to get out of bed
Anger tastes like raw meat
Like smelly, disgusting feet
Anger smells like cheese
That doesn't make you pleased
Anger looks like a puddle of blood splattered across the wall
Like Humpty's great fall
Anger feels like violence
But there is no silence
Anger reminds me of my mum
Like the horrendous smell that she lets out of her bum!

Danielle Foley (8)
Earlham Primary School, Forest Gate

Anger

Anger sounds like a bomb exploding
Anger tastes like sickly sweet peas
Anger smells like smelly donkeys
Anger looks like giant jaws
Anger is black
Anger reminds me of the Jaws theme song.

Alfie Cook (8)
Earlham Primary School, Forest Gate

Anger

Anger is red like a flashy traffic light
It sounds like a roaring lion
It feels like hot boiling water
It smells like a stinky bin
It tastes like salty, sour crisps
It reminds me of loneliness.

Samiha Begum
Earlham Primary School, Forest Gate

Anger

Anger is the colour of red
When your blood comes out of your head
Anger tastes like rotten bananas
Like worms coming out of sultanas
Anger smells like foxes
Wearing socks
Anger looks like bats
Wanting to hit cats
Anger feels like disappointment
Or going to the dentist's appointment
Anger reminds me of ghosts
Giving me notes.

Fabbiha Rahat Islam (8)
Earlham Primary School, Forest Gate

Happiness

Happiness sounds like your friends coming to your house
Happiness tastes like apple pie
Happiness smells like a bountiful fruit tree
Happiness feels like going to your friend's house
Happiness looks like a bountiful rainbow in the sky
Happiness reminds me of being kind to my sister, brother and friends.

Mikal Ana Lafronté (8)
Earlham Primary School, Forest Gate

Anger

Anger is red like a furious fire
It sounds like a thunderstorm
It feels like hot boiling water
It smells like a stinky nappy
It tastes like sour crisps
It reminds me of the day of punishment.

S Mohammed Hussain Nagvi (7)
Earlham Primary School, Forest Gate

Anger

Anger's colour is red
Anger sounds like lightning crashing through the clouds
Making my ears ache
Anger tastes like hot chilli making my throat explode
Anger smells like rotten, burning food on my plate
Anger feels like onions making my eyes weep
My throat getting soggy
Anger looks like my favourite toy being spoiled
By fruit juice with mustard on top
Anger reminds me of me getting bullied by two boys.

Aini Kamal (8)
Earlham Primary School, Forest Gate

Lonely

Being lonely sounds depressing and sad
It tastes like nothing but cold air
It smells of tears that have fallen from sad eyes
It looks like someone with no one with him or her
It feels lonely
It reminds me of a boy being lonely.

Ferdos Mohammed Ahmed (9)
Earlham Primary School, Forest Gate

Anger

Anger is like a red volcano
It sounds like a tank grenade
It feels like a glaring fire
It smells like rotten tomato
It tastes like sour lemon
It reminds me of the day of punishment.

Mohamed Saiamul Alam Saiam (7)
Earlham Primary School, Forest Gate

Anger

Anger is red like a furious fire
It sounds like a yelling baby
It feels like hot gleaming sunshine
It smells like burning toast
It tastes like sour milk
It reminds me of a day of sorrow.

Justina Kapociute (7)
Earlham Primary School, Forest Gate

Anger

Anger is like a red glaring fire
It sounds like a fierce volcano
It feels like the hot boiling sun
It smells like the stinky bin
It tastes like sour lemon
It reminds me of pain and agony.

Vitesh Dav (7)
Earlham Primary School, Forest Gate

Anger

Anger is red like a flashing set of traffic lights
It sounds like a shooting bonfire
It feels like burning parathas
It smells like a stinky bin
It tastes like burnt bread
It reminds me of Mum yelling at me.

Ameerah Rahman (7)
Earlham Primary School, Forest Gate

Anger

Anger sounds like a croaky voice
Anger tastes sour like vinegar
Anger smells of smoke
Anger looks like gorillas' teeth
Anger feels like a rock, rough and hard
Anger reminds me of my birthday
When I didn't get a present
It makes me feel angry!

Manzurul Islam (9)
Earlham Primary School, Forest Gate

Anger

Anger is red like a flashing fireball
It sounds like a loud thunderstorm
It smells like a stinky nappy
It tastes like a sour lemon
It feels like hot gleaming sunshine
It reminds me of the day of violence.

Mikal Vicente (7)
Earlham Primary School, Forest Gate

My Mum

My mum is very fun,
She always make nice lunch
And when I come home,
She gives me hugs.

Aisha Latif (6)
Forest School, Timperley

The Wind

The wind crashes and smashes its way through the land,
Leaving total destruction in its wake.
It picks up skyscrapers,
Then snaps them as easily as a toothpick.
It rips up the tarmac roads,   ·
Tearing them as easily as paper.
It bashes its way to the cliff,
Where the sea crashes against it.
It hurls massive boulders,
Trying to hit the fishing boats on the horizon.
But now the chilly night is over
And it settles back down,
Stomping back to its echoing cave to rest.
People's lives are in despair,
But as they try and repair,
They are desperately unaware,
Of the same danger that's dangling just above their heads!

Harry MacDonald (10)
Forest School, Timperley

The Wind

When the wind is howling between the buildings,
It's like a wolf hunting for food.

The wind gently carries a seed along,
Like a butterfly fluttering through the trees.

A soft, gentle breeze whispers
Through the tall trees.

A silent but deadly wind
Blows umbrellas inside out.

A long, powerful wind twisting and turning in every direction,
So powerful it snaps branches off trees.

A forceful wind dashes through the vent in your lounge,
For you to find the room freezing cold!

Kimberley Johal (10)
Forest School, Timperley

The Wind

When the wind is howling between buildings,
It's like a raging tornado angrily knocking down
Everything in its path.

When the wind is whispering through the trees,
It's like a fairy playing hide-and-seek
Sprinkling magic dust.

When the wind is carrying a dandelion seed along
It's like a colourful ribbon
Gliding with the warm breeze.

When the wind is flickering flames
It's like fireworks
Burning into the sky.

When the wind is making a cold draught in the house
It's like the ghost of the old owner
Calling from the depths of Hell.

Xouxhaenya Henry
Forest School, Timperley

The Wind

When the wind is howling through the buildings,
It's like the brutal behaviour of a lion in a cage.

When storming through the forest,
It's like a wolf tearing open its prey.

When the tornado's around,
It's like a cheetah moving quickly over the land.

But when it's carrying a dandelion seed along,
It's like a busy bee carrying the pollen to its hive.

And when it's silent and calm,
It's like an antelope swiftly crossing the country!

James Campbell (10)
Forest School, Timperley

The Wind

The wind can be like a wolf,
Howling at a glowing moon.

The wind can be like a mother,
Gently singing to her child.

The wind can be like leaves rustling,
On an ancient oak tree.

The wind can be like birds,
Twittering merrily in the treetops.

The wind can be like a lion roaring,
With anger and rage.

The wind can be like a swan,
Gliding across a lake.

The wind can be like an elephant,
Ripping trees out of the bone-dry dirt.

The wind can be like the waves,
Softly brushing against the sand.

James Farrow (10)
Forest School, Timperley

The Wind

The wind is a beast
Causing destruction over the land.
It crushes trees
And churns up seas,
Then clashes on the rocks.

The flocks of sheep,
Will not sleep,
As the violent wind howls,
So no children play,
Instead, they stay,
On the cold, windy day.

Edward Ward (10)
Forest School, Timperley

The Wind

When the wind is howling between the buildings,
It's like an eagle swooping in the sky looking for its prey.

It carries a dandelion seed along
Like somebody jumping off a cliff and parachuting down.

It breaks branches off the trees
To scare the butterflies and bees.

It whistles through the house
Making the air even colder.

It whispers through the trees with the bats drifting around it
Making it into a gentle breeze.

Now it breaks into a gale
Messing up the lawn, but by dawn
It is settled for people
To wake up and yawn.

Kelly Peters (10)
Forest School, Timperley

The Wind

The wind can come in all different ways
In breeze, gales and hurricanes
Your hair all over the place
The ruddy cheeks on your face
As soon as you get home, turn on the fire
When you relax, think of your desire.

If it stops
I would check your crops
And if they are damaged
They need to be managed
Now you are warm
Off goes the storm.

Katie Brayzier (10)
Forest School, Timperley

The Wind

When the wind howls on a cold winter's night
It's like wolves baying at the moon.

The cold draught feels like a ghost
Clambering up your spine.

Then, on a beautiful day, a gentle breeze carries a dandelion seed
Along like an antelope prancing on the plains.

Suddenly, a storm arrives, breaking branches
Like a lion snapping his foe's bones.

Then moves along and leaves no sound
Or movement behind.

Then everyone comes outside
Children play on their bikes.

But the wind is still there
Helping the children to ride along.

Georgina Nelson (10)
Forest School, Timperley

The Great Wind

The wind is howling through the buildings
Like the Devil screaming as he hears
The painful laughter from Heaven.

The wind is whispering through the trees,
Like a cheetah stealthily gliding in and out of the grass.

The wind is making a cold draught in the house
Like the icy cold winter spraying its poison throughout the land.

The wind is drifting a dandelion seed along
Like a butterfly swerving away from its predator.

The wind is breaking branches off a tree
Like an angry mob of baboons chasing the innocent monkeys.

Daniel Waxman (11)
Forest School, Timperley

Friends

A friend is someone who cares for me,
Friends are very kind to me,
Your best friend stays by your side,
Someone who is always there for you.

Sometimes we fall out and argue,
But before you know it, we're best friends again,
A friend does not tell lies to you,
A friend is fair to you.

My best friends do not fall out with me,
My best friends have fun and play with me,
They are to look after you,
My best friends are Edward, Kieran, Andreas and Ben.

My best friends tell me jokes,
When they come to tea, we always fall out,
But when they go, I always want them to stay,
But the following day, they are best friends with me.

George Johnston (8)
Forest School, Timperley

The Wind

The wind is like a wolf howling at the moon on a cold winter's night
It can be like a lion silently stalking its prey
It is like a bee gently flickering through the meadow
Sometimes, it is like a raging twirl, devouring everything that
                                                    stands in its way
The whistling wind swoops through the forest like an eagle
The wind is like an angry dog and rattles the windows with his paws
It leaps onto the roof and makes helpless sounds.
It carries a single dandelion along on the gentle breeze
It's like a fire's flickering flame that crackles in the moonlight
Finally, it starts to go down, to try and find another place to blow.

Lauren Richards (10)
Forest School, Timperley

The Wind

The wind is like a wolf howling at the full silver moon,
Then it disappears, but it will be back very soon.
The whistling wind sweeps through the forest
Like a fox stalking its prey,
It is very calm and sweet during the months of June and May.

When the wind taunts the raging sea,
The waves crash upon the shore,
The wind swirls and twirls around the empty house,
But cannot break through the door.
It swoops and glides along the floor,
It shouts at the fire asking for more.

The wind cries and cries for all to hear,
It slithers over a hill and startles a deer.
The month of May is nearly here,
It swoops up towards the sky and disappears.

Olivia Prickett (11)
Forest School, Timperley

Friends

A friend is someone who's kind
Who helps you clear your mind
Someone who always helps you
Someone who's always there.

Connor Rutherford (7)
Forest School, Timperley

Friends

A friend is someone that helps you
Someone who is always there
It does not matter if I don't get my way
We always help each other.

Amy Connell (7)
Forest School, Timperley

The Wind

The wind is howling through the dark,
Like a wolf and his beastly bark,
The wind creeps through the trees,
Like swallows' wings making a cool breeze,
It makes a gentle swishing sound,
Like bees hiding in flowers, waiting to be found,
It's like a roasting, flickering fire,
Like someone's cackling laughter.

Blowing umbrellas inside out,
Like a deer racing through the trees,
It makes a cool, refreshing breeze,
Carrying leaves throughout the land,
Like droplets landing on the sand,
Snapping branches off a tree,
Like from a cage, a lion breaking free.

Alison Poon (10)
Forest School, Timperley

Untitled

A friend is someone who helps me
Someone who's always there
A friend is someone who helps you when you're sad
And takes you to the teacher

A friend is someone who likes me
And plays with you every day
A friend is someone kind
And helps me all the way

Someone who is happy
Is the right friend for me
Who helps me when I'm feeling sad
And listens to me.

Edward Galley (7)
Forest School, Timperley

Friends

A friend is someone who cares for me,
Someone who's always there,
Sometimes we fall out and argue,
But I don't really care.

Because we always make it up again,
A friend is someone who is fair,
My best friend is always by my side,
It is Amy.

Rebecca Greaves (7)
Forest School, Timperley

Friends

A friend is someone who helps me
She smiles every time I see her
I sit next to her in class time
And invite her round for tea.

Olivia Baldwin (7)
Forest School, Timperley

Friends

A friend is someone special who always helps me
And if we fall out, we come back together,
If she or he will come back together,
We will still be friends forever.

Abigail Turner (7)
Forest School, Timperley

Friends

A friend is someone who helps me,
Someone who's always there,
Someone who never bosses me,
Someone who is fair!

Sometimes we start to argue,
Sometimes we fall out,
Everyone gets a bit bossy,
But does not mind!
My friend is always there!

Sana Naik (7)
Forest School, Timperley

Friends

When I invite them for tea
They sometimes fall out with me
We try to forget all about it
And in the end, we go home as friends.

Kieren Sharma (7)
Forest School, Timperley

Friends

My best friend is Thomas,
Because he makes me laugh,
I've had him by my side for years,
I like it when he comes for tea.

Jack Fisher (7)
Forest School, Timperley

The Wind

A man, maybe a ghost, but everyone knows this is the wind
When he's angry, he swirls, roars and rages
He makes the sea crash and clash, trying to fight the dreadful wind
Whispering compared to the wind
Screaming in the sea's ear
He rips at the trees not listening to their protests
Laughing at the oaks and beeches
Ignoring the screams of the pines and sycamores
And cackling at the plants and flowers
When the wind is unhappy, he slowly glides back
To his dark, echoing cave
Hanging his head and short bursts of wind
Coming from his tear ducts
But soon he will be out again -
Lured by the sound of children laughing
When the wind feels mischievous he blows breezes through houses
Blowing fires out with just one snort
When he chuckles he makes people's spines tingle
But when he is happy he laughs and dances
Making leaves rustle and branches sway
When he calms down, he lies in a field
And makes the corn blow from side to side
And carries a dandelion seed along
He laughs and slowly drifts off on a breeze.

Giulia Baggaley Simpson (10)
Forest School, Timperley

The Wind

The wind is controlled by the stars at night,
Breaking branches with elemental power beaming from the sky.
The wind furiously rages through the land, devastating the future,
The power of wind is like an erupting volcano darkening the sky.
The wind has joined forces with a mystic power from ancient time,
All motion of life has been demolished, but only God stays standing.

Chetan Dusara (10)
Forest School, Timperley

The Beach

As I walk across the cliff
Down to the beach
I hear the stones of all shapes and sizes
Chatter to one another
As the crashing waves fall upon them
Sandcastles are drowned
As the foamy waves creep up the beach
Playful dolphins jump and dance in the bay
As the sun sets, everybody leaves the beach
I stand there all alone
A pirate ship sails away beyond the horizon
I look up
Stars twinkle above my head
It's magical.

Roslyn Harrion (8)
Hazeldown Primary School, Teignmouth

My Cats

My cats leap around without a care
Chasing mice here and there
My cats are always adventurous
They are never furious
My cats are never late for eating food
But always in a good mood
My cats fight over who should eat their food first
They eat so much, you'd think they would burst
My cats aren't really that bad
In fact, I'm very glad, to have cats like mine
My cats are wonderful!

Anastasia Weston (8)
Hazeldown Primary School, Teignmouth

Acorn Man

Acorn man is by my side
Rushing through the acorn tide
Take off your hat and look around
Because acorn man has come to town.

Squirrels come to steal the nuts
So watch out, acorn man, don't fear the cut.

Mikey Evans (8)
Hazeldown Primary School, Teignmouth

My Pussycat - Haiku

Big, chubby pussy,
Eating fish and meaty things,
Ginger cuddly cat.

Annie Salter (8)
Hazeldown Primary School, Teignmouth

Big Bee - Haiku

Yellow bumblebee
Prancing around pretty plants
Searching for nectar.

Georgia McGrane (8)
Hazeldown Primary School, Teignmouth

Waterfall - Haiku

Gushing waterfall
Splashing, crashing water waves
Refreshing cool breeze.

Amy Broderick (8)
Hazeldown Primary School, Teignmouth

My Dog - Haikus

My dog likes playing
He always wags his tail fast
My dog runs around

Jumps on the settee
He springs on the trampoline
I like him so much

My dog is so mad
We take him out on a walk
That's my favourite thing

My dog's got patches
He has got spots on his nose
He is black and white.

Jessica Morris (8)
Hazeldown Primary School, Teignmouth

Christmas - Haikus

Christmas is so great
You get hundreds of presents
I like pirate ships!

Christmas is funny
You get thousands of sweets now
I like toffee pie!

Turkey for Christmas
Christmas pudding for pudding
I am full up now!

Daniel Harvey (8)
Hazeldown Primary School, Teignmouth

Hallowe'en

Spiders on the floor
Witches flying out in the sky
Ghosts making noises

People making pumpkins
Bats flying in the dark sky
Poisons exploding

Skeletons hanging
People running far away
I'm a little witch.

Sophy Moyle (8)
Hazeldown Primary School, Teignmouth

The Bully

There's a bully at my school,
But he thinks he is really cool,
He whacks that smile off your face,
With his big guitar case,
He always makes us cry,
Like we are about to die,
He thinks he is really tall,
But in fact, he is really small.

Lurie Moore (8)
Hazeldown Primary School, Teignmouth

Tiger Cub

There's a tiger cub
Pouncing above the grass
Then sees Mum and has a little drink
Off again, running with milk all over his face
Then he goes to her den
As nightfall comes.

Emily Northcott (8)
Hazeldown Primary School, Teignmouth

Football

I like football
Football is great
Shoot, shoot, goal, goal!

Run, run, dodge, dodge!
Tackle, tackle, tackle!
Run through the players
Shoot
Goal!

Samuel Speed (9)
Hazeldown Primary School, Teignmouth

Hallowe'e' - Haikus

Hallowe'en is fun
Trick or treating down the road
Pumpkins are scary

Hallowe'en has ghosts
Hallowe'en has skeletons
People in costumes.

Jazmine White (9)
Hazeldown Primary School, Teignmouth

Squirrel

They are tree-dwellers
Scuttling up in the trees
Squirrels are the best.

I love grey and red
But red are still my favourite
I still love them so.

Matthew Brooks (8)
Hazeldown Primary School, Teignmouth

Rainforest

R ain dripping
A sleep snakes
I cky-sticky tree juice
N aughty piranhas sucking blood
F reezing rivers totally white
O pen rivers racing
R acing rivers racing through the rainforest
E ating animals and cracking bones
S nakes shedding their skins
T errifying tigers attacking.

Will Kelly (8)
Hazeldown Primary School, Teignmouth

Nature Poem

F oxes hunting for food
O wls sleeping in the comfortable nest
R abbits in cosy burrows
E agles soaring overhead
S wallows in the shady woods
T iny creatures searching for food.

Tom Libby (8)
Hazeldown Primary School, Teignmouth

In The Big Forest

F rosty leaves of ice and snow
O wls silently sleeping in the old trees
R esting salmon in the long, calm river
E astern fluffy foxes loudly howling
S wallows quietly hunting for some tasty food
T awny owls silently smelling for food.

Matthew Shimell (8)
Hazeldown Primary School, Teignmouth

Lions

Lion sleeping in the jungle
You can hear his great rumble
Eating meat, getting blood everywhere
He will eat just anywhere
Planning tricks and fighting creatures
He's got so many hairy features
Huge and furry, big, long mane
He isn't really very tame.

Holly Reed (8)
Hazeldown Primary School, Teignmouth

Dog

My dog is funny and makes me laugh
He loves playing with his toys
My favourite thing is walking him.

I walk him up to the shop
I play with him in our back garden
His favourite toy is his bouncy ball.

Sophie Rainbow (8)
Hazeldown Primary School, Teignmouth

In The Forest

F rosty leaves of snow and ice
O ld leaves falling off the trees
R esting fishes in the calm lake
E ggs of a robin cramped in a nest
S limy fish swimming around
T iny bugs crawling around.

Sam Peat (8)
Hazeldown Primary School, Teignmouth

My Favourite Worst Things

'Mum, can I have a biscuit?'
'No!'
'Not even a crumb?'
'No, not even a crumb!'

'Mum, can I have a pet?'
'No!'
'Not even an ant?'
'No, not even an ant!'

'Mum, can I watch TV?'
'No!'
'Not even for a second?'
'No, not even for a second!'

'Mum, can I go to school?'
'No!'
'But it's against the law!'
'So?'

'Mum, can I have a kiss?'
'Yes, of course!'
'That's strange!'

Helena Cope (8)
Hazeldown Primary School, Teignmouth

My Kitten

My kitten flies out the window
Into the garden
Skids in the kitchen, runs into my room
Bites other cats' tails, follows me to the loo
He's a nose basher, bite master!

My kitten is a hungry kitten
A pop star cat
He is a cheeky kitten
He likes to play football.

Jack Phillips (8)
Hazeldown Primary School, Teignmouth

My Bike

My bike's so fast,
Riding down a hill,
Zooming past the houses,
Riding on the road.

Wheels spinning,
Round and round,
Faster than a car,
Riding on my bike,
It's really fun.

Jake Peat (8)
Hazeldown Primary School, Teignmouth

Football

Football's great
You take a shot
From a free kick
And score a goal
In the back of the net
And the crowd goes
Wild!

Christopher Johnson (8)
Hazeldown Primary School, Teignmouth

Monster

A hungry monster
A naughty monster
Chasing my sister round the town.
Eats her up
Yuck!
He doesn't like the taste of my sister!

Jordan Pocock (8)
Hazeldown Primary School, Teignmouth

The Teacher-Eating Plant

Out in the grounds,
The teacher-eating plant's body is as big as a boulder,
Teeth bared - that's why the grounds are deserted.
A teacher went missing and was found
At the bottom of the plant, where the roots were vibrating.

Whilst out on duty, she'd smelt something fruity
And stepped the wrong way -
Snap, crackle and *crunch, hey, hey,*
'What a miserable day,' I say.

They put a fence around it,
To totally surround it,
You can still see it today,
But beware, stay away!

Callum Booker (8)
Hazeldown Primary School, Teignmouth

Jungle - Haiku

Hot sticky jungle
Enormous banana leaves
Smelling fragrances.

Alisha-Mae Aplin (8)
Hazeldown Primary School, Teignmouth

The Rainy Forest

I can hear the pitter-patter of the wet rain
I can see the dark black clouds above my head
I can smell the freshness of the cold rain
I can taste the stormy winter coming
I can feel the freezing wind against my soft face.

Adam Lee (8)
Hazeldown Primary School, Teignmouth

My Favourite Thing Is My Puppy, Oscar

Oscar is mad, puppy-like
Oscar's messy, chewing everything
Mucky Oscar licking me!

Puppy says, 'Hello!'
Oscar is a crazy puppy
Not to mention, mad.

Oscar's ticklish
Licking me on the mouth, *urgh!*
Oscar's a greedy dog!

Erin Hodgson (8)
Hazeldown Primary School, Teignmouth

My Cat Myrtle - Haiku

Silky soft, loves hugs
Zippy, running all around
Topsy-turvy cat.

Ellen Bryan (8)
Hazeldown Primary School, Teignmouth

My Favourite Thing

My puppy is funny
My puppy is cute
My puppy plays with me
She even goes to sleep with me
But she isn't there in the morning
So puppy, come and play with me.

Leigh-Anne Preston (8)
Hazeldown Primary School, Teignmouth

My Weird Classroom

My weird classroom
Is really weird
The doorknob is shaped like an eel
When you walk in, you will see a fright
Children fighting, day and night
In my classroom are lots of creatures
Flying frogs and dancing leeches
Then the windows open and close
How they do it? Nobody knows
Next, the desks that move around
My desk can be rarely found
Then the pencils that move on their own
No one holding them
They write on their own
But the weirdest thing is
That the teacher's chair
Is a toilet
But no one cares!

Luke Bishop (10)
Lipson Vale Primary School, Lipson

My Family

I have a grandad that snores,
A sister that falls,
A mum that never takes a joke,
A brother that does folk,
A cat that smells,
A friend that tells,
A snail that smiles,
Who goes miles,
You don't want to meet my family!

Francesca Griffiths (10)
Lipson Vale Primary School, Lipson

The Cloakroom

What can you find down there?
You might find something very rare,
Maybe a stone
Or a very shiny bone,
Bread from France,
Some old teacher's pants,
Something smiley,
An old welly,
You might find a witch's broom,
In the school's cloakroom!

Rachel Miller (10)
Lipson Vale Primary School, Lipson

Going To School

Getting dressed in a rush
Mum telling you to hush
Opening the door
Work falling on the floor
Going to the gate
And I will be late
We know you're stressed
But why aren't you dressed?

Faye West (10)
Lipson Vale Primary School, Lipson

Hannah

There was a young girl named Hannah
Who loved to sing songs of Susannah
She had a headache
So she ate a whole cake
Still, she's as thin as a spanner!

Laura Farley (10)
Lipson Vale Primary School, Lipson

Oops!

Oops, oops, I did it again,
I broke my teacher's favourite pen.
Oops, oops, I'm really sorry,
I broke my friend's favourite lorry.
Oops, oops, this is the worst by far,
I broke my dad's brand new car.
Oops, oops, I'm going to die,
I ate my sister's last piece of pie.
Oops, oops, it's all my fault,
I killed the cat with too much salt.
Oops, oops, it wasn't nice,
I turned my mouse to solid ice.
Oops, oops, why was I born?
I'm as useful as jeans all torn!

Sam Bailey (11)
Lipson Vale Primary School, Lipson

What Could It Be?

It's never-ending
It's everlasting
It has no beginning
And no ending
It's made by atoms
Quickly moving objects
Move inside it
Just too much of it
To put in one poem
Not enough of it
To put on a page.

The universe.

Jessica Mallory (10)
Lipson Vale Primary School, Lipson

RSPCA

Young dogs, young cats,
Need our help,
They really need a new and better home,
There is a future out there waiting for them.

Just a little food,
In need of warm blankets and clean water,
They are rescued from abuse,
Their past is but their future.

We can help them if we try,
It doesn't take much to help,
All it takes is tender love
And a piece of your heart.

Elland Hawker (10)
Lipson Vale Primary School, Lipson

My Test

I was sitting at my desk
And my teacher said,
'Hand in your test.'
I turned around and said,
'You little pest.'
'What?' she shrieked,
'Nothing, Miss,' I cried.
When I got home, I shouted,
'You little thing, you ate half of my test!'
'Quite right!' he replied,
For he is the Crazy Frog.

Gemma Humphrey (10)
Lipson Vale Primary School, Lipson

School

School, school, is always boring,
When I'm in maths, I'm always snoring.
I hate my work I do at school,
But if I don't do it, I'm the biggest fool.
Sometimes school is really fun,
Sometimes we even get a bun.
Sometimes in PE,
Miss always picks on me,
School, school, is always boring,
I can't believe that I'm always snoring!

Michaella Toombs-Dunleavy (10)
Lipson Vale Primary School, Lipson

What Am I?

Fast-runner
Great-killer
Good-swimmer
Long-tail
Brilliant-sneaker
Loud-roarer
Thick-fur

What am I?
A snow leopard.

Sam Carey (10)
Lipson Vale Primary School, Lipson

Man U

Man U, Man U, they are they best
Who I think is better than the rest
Wayne Rooney scored a goal
Now he's broken his toe
But now he's wearing a vest.

Macauley Cole (10)
Lipson Vale Primary School, Lipson

The Day I Got Lost In A Supermarket

It was another boring Sunday
And shopping had just begun!

First, we visited the fruit and veg
And in our trolley lay:
Carrots, peas, sweetcorn and . . .
Yuck! Brussels sprouts!
And don't forget the bananas and grapes.

Then we entered the clothes
And bought loads of drapes.

Then came a toaster, a phone
And a loaf of bread.

I went to look at the toys
And found a gang of boys!

'Mum, where are you?'
It started to get late
And suddenly, they closed the gates!

That was it, I was doomed,
So then, off I zoomed,
This way, that way,
There was nothing to do.

I was lost!

Here I camped in the toilet roll section,
I had to make a house
And at the break of dawn
I started to yawn
And before me stood . . .
My mum!

(I was home!)

Erin Crisp (10)
Lipson Vale Primary School, Lipson

The War

It was a cold night as the large aircraft
Silently cruised above the sand, cities and war.
The war was everywhere, missiles shooting
Loud bangs and cracks from explosions and other large weapons.
The worst was the thunder of noise from above
As the aircraft shot out the huge balls of metal.
They were like vehicles with turrets of rockets blasting out from inside
As we landed, the door flung open, so we grabbed a gun
And our kit, got to the bunker and fired.
The flares we shot over, lit up lorries, tanks and men.
Hundreds of men, we could see lights from the guns they were using.
You only heard bangs, cracks and the worst of all was the screams,
Screams of men in agony from when they were shot
Some had no arms or legs, but you had to see it
And fight until your time ran out.

Curtis Young (10)
Lipson Vale Primary School, Lipson

The Environment Monster

The howling wind danced by the colourful growing flowers,
Birds sang sweets songs like a record player over and over again,
The insects and bugs ran freely through the bright green grass,
It was a beautiful day.

Until suddenly, the tiny creatures heard a loud *boom!*
The disturbing sound came from a tall human, a giant,
The poor animals let out a screeching cry
As they got squashed under a huge shoe.

Our environment gets ruined every day,
Pick up your rubbish and take it away!

Connie Jane Veale (10)
Lipson Vale Primary School, Lipson

Save The Tigers

Orange and black giants creeping in the grass,
Big yellow eyes staring into space,
Paws the size of my hands,
Save the tigers!

Long, pure-white whiskers,
Twitching at every sign of movement,
Thick camouflage fur, swaying in the breeze,
Bulging body, ready to pounce out,
Save the tigers!

Wait a minute, what's that?
Leaves crunching, grass rustling,
Bang! Bang!
Save the tigers!

Maddy Luxton (10)
Lipson Vale Primary School, Lipson

Autism In Their Eyes

People coming, people going,
But the Devil chose you,
You're stuck with a curse,
That know one can lift, but why?

The screams that you yell,
They're relentless,
But you keep struggling,
On and on.

The anger you may be filled with,
Trapped in a box you can't be let free,
Your parents are, but why not you?
Yet you're still living.

Hannah Wills (10)
Lipson Vale Primary School, Lipson

Football

Football is a beautiful game
Where the crowd in the stands
Shout and scream
As their team score a goal

The pitch is empty after the game
When all the crowd have gone
There is only the stadium manager and his staff
That check the pitch for any rubbish or problems

The players leave in their fancy cars
To go to their posh homes
With their wives or friends
Or even their children

As the sky turns black
The stadium has been checked
With everything closed
For training in the morning

Every Saturday, it happens again.

Alexander Pethick (11)
Lipson Vale Primary School, Lipson

Nemo

Scratch, scratch, on the door
My pet cat is like a boar
My front door is getting sore
Nemo keeps scratching more and more
He just won't stop
So I give him a bop
On his head
Then he goes straight to bed
Scratch, scratch, on the door
My pet cat is like a boar.

Kate Sands (10)
Lipson Vale Primary School, Lipson

My Mum

My mum's funny
Inside and out
When someone tells a joke
She gives a big shout
She's got curly hair
And always is fair
When she's doing a dare
My mum's cool
And always will be.

Evelyn Francis (10)
Lipson Vale Primary School, Lipson

What Am I?

Loud-sleeper
Lazy-worker
Sofa-lover
TV-hogger
Garbage-smeller
Mega-wild

What am I?
I'm a man.

Deanna Pealing (10)
Lipson Vale Primary School, Lipson

The Remarkable Hamster

I had a hamster called Teeny
Who was a little bit weeny
He was very clever
And predicted the weather
He now wears a blue bikini!

Fern Buller (10)
Lipson Vale Primary School, Lipson

Love

Love is like a teddy bear,
Flowing through the air,
Love blows at your cheeks,
Every couple of weeks,
Love is like a river,
When you walk, you shiver,
Love is always in your heart,
Going to marry in a cart.

Charlotte Goodchild (10)
Lipson Vale Primary School, Lipson

Who Am I?

My ears are like a pointed cactus
Claws are like shark's teeth
My tail is a grumpy snake
My whiskers are hard string
My teeth are sharper than pins
My nose is a wet pink button
My fur is like a teddy bear
My paws are bigger than a man's hand.

Aimee Rayner-Okines (9)
Oaklands Primary School, Welwyn

Senses

I wish my nose was a rocket
I wish my eye was a planet
I wish my tongue was a star
I wish my hand was an astronaut
I wish my ear was a Saturn ring.

Emily Lauran Stacey (8)
Oaklands Primary School, Welwyn

Spacecraft

All space vehicles moving
Every person floating
Now astronauts going back
A crew are stuck!
Now everything slows down.

The crews move again
Some rockets going fast
An astronaut helper going across
An alien walking on the moon
Every teacher in space . . . jumping about.

David Ackland (7)
Oaklands Primary School, Welwyn

A Cat

Ears like mini mountains
A nose as wet as a lake
A body like a big fur ball
He has a tail like a snake
He has claws as sharp as pencil lead.

Who am I?

George James Wallis-Smith (9)
Oaklands Primary School, Welwyn

My Dog Gemma

Her fur is as soft as a thousand pillows
Her paws are as black as the sky at midnight
Her teeth are as sharp as thorns
Her eyes are horse chestnuts.

Holly Swinburne (8)
Oaklands Primary School, Welwyn

Ancient Egypt

A ncient Egypt is so glorious
N ever to be seen or known
C urious smells in the air really making you cunning
I nformation from everywhere going to the heart
E gypt is richer than you thought
N owhere in the whole of Egypt will a mummy be seen
T angling vines in all the pyramids

E gypt is such a wonderful place to live
G entle sun swaying over the land
Y ou would live a long life there
P ut everything in the sand and it slowly, softly sinks
T ender bandages wrapped around the mummies.

Robert Drew (8)
Oaklands Primary School, Welwyn

Animals

A nimals are cute and love a cuddle
N ever any trouble
I n the house they leave a wet puddle
M ake lots of mess every minute
A nimals love playing with you all the time
L ove a stroke from time to time
S illy pets are so much fun.

Zara Hoy (8)
Oaklands Primary School, Welwyn

Sport

S port is the best of the best
P eople love sport so much
O h yes they do
R ooney is so good at football
T he greatest thing in the world is sport.

Will Vaughan (8)
Oaklands Primary School, Welwyn

Dolphins

D olphins like to jump around and play
O n an unusual day
L ay low when nobody knows
P ose when the wind blows
H eroes and heroines I suppose
I nstead they know the water flows
N ow we only see a flick of their nose
S ee the people when they row.

Philippa Stephens (8)
Oaklands Primary School, Welwyn

Families

F amilies are fun and kind
A family cares for you
M aking people laugh
I love my mum and dad
L aughter and joking from my brother and me
Y ou share stuff from your cousins.

Megan Jackson (7)
Oaklands Primary School, Welwyn

Families

F amilies are fun
A family will make you happy
M um, Dad and me all cosy
I love my family
L ove is the best
Y ou, me, Mum and Dad.

Niamh Whicher & Renée Beane (7)
Oaklands Primary School, Welwyn

Race Car

R acing on the track
A cross the world race like mad
C ars crashing on the side
E asy for the experts

C lattering like crazy
A dventuring along the tracks
R acing for the finish.

Adam Webster (8)
Oaklands Primary School, Welwyn

My Fox, Firefly

Her fur is flickering fire,
Her ears are as pricked as a beak,
Her nose is a black button,
Her paws are soft sponges,
Her teeth are like white pearls,
Her claws are deadly knives.

Eleanor Smith (9)
Oaklands Primary School, Welwyn

The Tiger

Fur like burnt grass
Claws as sharp as knives
His teeth are stalactites and stalagmites
His eyes are like orange fire
A tail lashing around.

Who am I?

James Firth (9)
Oaklands Primary School, Welwyn

Who Am I?

My fur feels like a brand new white teddy
My nose is a big black button
Ears are snowy mountains
My paws are like moon boots
My eyes are like two black holes
Who am I?

I am a polar bear.

Lucy Reynolds (9)
Oaklands Primary School, Welwyn

The Dog

Ears like velvety waterfalls coming down,
A tail like a whip,
His paws are squishy sponges,
His claws are like pins,
His eyes are as round as marbles,
His teeth are porcupine spikes,
His fur is as fluffy as Santa's beard.

Maxwell Brendish (9)
Oaklands Primary School, Welwyn

The Hawk

His hearing is as sharp as a pin,
A tail as straight as a ruler,
His feather are scales,
His eyes are like two flames flickering in the dark,
His beak is the yellow sun,
His claws are as sharp as a cactus.

Amanveer Benning (9)
Oaklands Primary School, Welwyn

Winter

The snow skates across the river,
Like a gleaming ice ring,
Winter awakes.

The snow falls from the sparkling trees,
Like a toddler taking its first steps and fails,
Winter is fading slowly.

A snowman frowns,
Standing alone in the mist,
Like a boy with no friends,
Winter dozes.

Josh Genever (11)
Oaklands Primary School, Welwyn

Spring

Lilies smell lovely, all different colours,
Orange, pink and white, all brightly coloured,
You can find them all over the world in people's gardens and houses,
Now it's winter, the lilies have gone,
They'll come back next year,
With more bright colours.

Naomi Baycroft (7)
Oaklands Primary School, Welwyn

My Taste

I wish I could eat a yummy cake
But afterwards I would have a tummy ache
Once I am in bed, I can have a yummy milkshake
I wish I could eat more cake
To see whether I would get another tummy ache
So I could have more milkshake every day.

Delorice Murudzwa (8)
Oaklands Primary School, Welwyn

Summer

Summer awakes,
Shining its gleaming head,
Like a long-lost memory
Forgotten.

Summer yawns,
Drifting from its sleepy break,
Like chirping birds stretching,
Awoken.

Summer pierces,
Freshly cut grass,
Like a rainbow on the greenish grass,
It is over again.

Samuel Borrie (10)
Oaklands Primary School, Welwyn

Giraffe

Its neck is a tall tree
Its ears are as dark as brown wood
Its body is a spotty cheetah
Its legs are like long, wavy branches
Its eyes are as bright as shining lights.

Elizabeth Spear (9)
Oaklands Primary School, Welwyn

A Hedgehog

A spiky ball when he curls up,
His eyes are like small snail shells,
His claws are like pins,
His teeth are mini diggers in his little mouth.

Hannah Young (9)
Oaklands Primary School, Welwyn

Summer

The flower dances,
Waves in the warm tepid wind,
Like a bright, wavy ribbon,
Summer's awake!

The sun blazes,
Lighting the pretty sky,
Like a glowing bright fire,
Summer's light!

The warm air breathes,
Blowing the coloured plants,
Like a very fast fan,
Summer's heat!

The lake shimmers,
Gazing at the hot sun,
Like a reflection in the mirror,
Summer ends!

Oliver Stephens (10)
Oaklands Primary School, Welwyn

Squirrel

His ears are like swivelling radar,
His teeth are chisels,
His eyes are like the stars,
His paws are tiny vices,
His tail is like a feather duster,
His fur is a dusty path in the desert.

Charlotte Birtles (9)
Oaklands Primary School, Welwyn

Night

The night arises
As the moon follows
Like newborn babies
With their mother swallows

The lights go out
In a blink of an eye
Like the sun descending
As daylight dies

The dead of the night
With the moonlight beam
Like a torch being shone
But nothing could be seen

When the night is tired
The sun will arise
Like a mouse coming out of its hole
With clear blue skies.

Richard Vaughan (10)
Oaklands Primary School, Welwyn

Who Am I?

His ears are as soft as silk beds,
His tail is as bright as the sun,
His nose is a black sponge,
His mouth is as slobbery as a bucket of water,
His eyes are as black as a rain cloud
His paws are as fluffy as mittens.

Sarah Cox (9)
Oaklands Primary School, Welwyn

The Fire's Heat

The fire stretches
Waking its deadly heart,
Glowing red like anger
Flickering.

The fire waves
Spreads its fiery tips,
Like on hot toast
Sparks.

The fire breathes
Blasting its smoking grey breath,
Like melting ice cream
Pops.

The fire settles
Snuggling down to go to bed,
Like a baby dozing off to sleep
Grows.

Luke Fuller (10)
Oaklands Primary School, Welwyn

The Polar Bear

His nose is blacker than the dark sky,
He has two bright stars flickering in the dark,
His fur is as white as snow,
His ears are pointy mountains,
His claws are like shark's teeth,
His teeth are sharp razors.

Harry Ironton (9)
Oaklands Primary School, Welwyn

Winter

Winter stretches,
Opening its arms,
Like a mother and a newborn baby,
Only the beginning.

Winter's coldness,
Awakens from a deep slumber,
Like a long-lost memory,
Recalled.

Winter remembers its chilly voice,
It remembers many things now,
Like a man returning from war,
Freezing cold.

Winter dies,
Spring is coming,
Like a relay runner passing the baton,
Spring has arrived.

Ryan O'Driscoll (10)
Oaklands Primary School, Welwyn

Giraffe

His fur is a Roman mosaic,
Ears as blank as paper,
Neck as long as a tree,
His legs kick like a horse,
His fur is a patchwork pattern,
Legs as strong as an elephant.

Harvey Turner (9)
Oaklands Primary School, Welwyn

The Moon

The moon gleams,
Creeps out at night,
Like a sudden flash,
Moonlight.

The moon shines,
Gazes on the Earth,
Like an enormous ball,
A sudden boom.

The moon sleeps,
Relaxes before going to bed,
Like a sleeping child,
A sudden snore.

The moon awakens,
Rests through the night,
Like listening to music,
A great likeness.

Robert White (9)
Oaklands Primary School, Welwyn

Elephant

The tusks are like rams on a ship,
A body is a stretched limo,
His trunk is a flexible snake,
His feet are like skyscrapers,
Its ears are like Sky dishes,
One toe is one pencil case.

Sulaimaan Mughal (9)
Oaklands Primary School, Welwyn

The Moon

The moon creeps,
Scaring all the glistening stars,
Like a stinking boat,
Tired.

The moon yawns,
Carefully, he wakes up,
Like a bear cub opening its eyes,
Weary.

The moon stares,
Watching the tired people beneath,
Like a cuckoo clock ticking,
Asleep.

The moon smiles,
Realising it's time to doze,
Like a tired baby,
He slumbers.

Hannah Kempster (10)
Oaklands Primary School, Welwyn

Red Kite

Its beak is a pair of scissors
Its feathers are as red as blood
Its claws are as sharp as knives
Its eyes are like glowing torches
Its wings are as wide as a canyon
It darts for its prey like a bullet
And soars triumphantly back to the skies above.

Samuel Curtis (9)
Oaklands Primary School, Welwyn

The Moon

The moon glows,
Taking over the bright day,
Like eyelids over eyes,
Night-time.

The moon gazes,
Peering over the blue and green Earth,
Like a nose leaning over a mouth,
Midnight.

The moon runs,
Around the colourful planets,
Like a baby's first steps,
Orbiting.

The moon shape shifts
In the beautiful sky,
Like a human growing,
Dawn.

George Ironton (10)
Oaklands Primary School, Welwyn

My Cat Tigger

My ears are pointed mountains,
My tail is a beating drum,
My paws are white boots,
My fur is a cuddly pillow,
My eyes are glowing light,
My teeth are pointed needles,
My nose is a pink button.

Katie Deards (8)
Oaklands Primary School, Welwyn

Tree

The tree yawns
Stretches its withered arms
Like a bewildered creature
Awakening.

The tree chuckles
Remembering distant memories
Like a tranquil secret
Deep inside the forest.

The tree blooms
Exquisite blossoms gracefully opening
Like an albatross spreading its wings
Forest smiles.

The tree slumbers
Embracing leaves turning brown
Like an ancient predecessor
The axe has come.

Emily Beswick (10)
Oaklands Primary School, Welwyn

My Pet Cat

Her ears are sharp stars,
The tail is like a hook,
The paws and claws are like a cactus,
Her body is like a zebra,
Her eyes are as cute as squirrel's eyes,
The teeth are like pencils getting sharper and sharper.

Nathan Donnelly (8)
Oaklands Primary School, Welwyn

Fire

Fire flickers,
Waking up, out of bed,
Like a chainsaw cutting down a hill,
Burning bright.

Fire prances,
Grazes leaves and scorches twigs,
Crackling like sausages in a frying pan
Steadily getting stronger.

Fire blazes,
Roaring above trees,
Like a lion yawning flames
The fire is alive.

Fire fades,
Slowly getting smaller,
Like a candle running out of wax,
Reduced to ash.

Matthew Walton (9)
Oaklands Primary School, Welwyn

The Tiger

His ears are a point on a triangle,
His nose is an orange sponge,
His fur is like patterns on a collage,
His eyes are like the bright sun,
His tail is a long, thin snake
And his mouth is a deep, black hole.

Laura Goodacre (8)
Oaklands Primary School, Welwyn

The Ocean

The ocean crashes,
Washing away the sand,
Like a person kicking a ball,
Animals flinch.

The ocean shifts,
Churning its blue, rough surface,
Like a person rolling his tongue,
Seamen hide.

The ocean destroys,
Pounding ships with almighty power,
Like bullies hurting children,
Ships sink.

The ocean calms,
Slowing, smoothing,
Like the grass swaying in the breeze,
Night falls.

Robert Vaughan (10)
Oaklands Primary School, Welwyn

A Squirrel

His tail is like a toilet brush,
His eyes are black buttons,
His ears are like mountains,
His claws are like vampire fangs,
His fur is like a grey, fluffy fur coat,
His whiskers are like guitar strings.

Ben Wilson (8)
Oaklands Primary School, Welwyn

Winter

Winter wakes
Freezes everybody in sight
Like a flash of lightning
The winter's just cold

A tree breathes
It waves its icy branches
Like an animal in a cage
Trying to escape

Frost creeps
Covers all the snowy cars
Like a caved human
The darkness is too strong

Winter sleeps
Coldness gently fading
Like fog disappearing
It gets warmer, we are at winter's end.

Daniel Hughes (10)
Oaklands Primary School, Welwyn

Fire

The fire wakes,
Waving at surprised people,
Like good friends,
Bright colours.

The fire jumps,
Dancing on burning wood,
Like a talented break dancer,
Sparkling ashes.

The fire sleeps,
Yawning while leaving,
Like a creeping rat,
Light fades.

Mark Wong (10)
Oaklands Primary School, Welwyn

Fire!

Fire awakes,
Fire screams across the lakes,
Fire speaks, it roars across the sky,
Fire waves as it passes by.

Fire relaxes when it leaps,
Fire can burn your keeps,
Fire tenses when you cry,
Fire creates infernos, then you die.

Fire lashes, it slams on you,
Fire can stop at nothing, it has no queue,
Fire flashes before your eyes,
Fire can't stop, it will leave you paralysed.

Fire now quietens, then it sleeps,
Fire has been tamed, it no longer creeps,
Fire dies, the water cries victory!
Fire is now dead, it now becomes sleepy . . .

Connor Wilson (10)
Oaklands Primary School, Welwyn

Spring

Spring alerts,
Rousing the opening flowers,
Like a calling mother,
Spring awakes.

Spring appears,
Peeping through the blooming bushes,
Like a playful child,
Growing old.

Spring dozes,
Sprawled on the brightly coloured grass,
Like a lazy boy sleeping,
Spring fades.

Shannee Rogers (10)
Oaklands Primary School, Welwyn

Winter Wakes

Winter rolls,
Moving in its icy bed,
Like a large black thunder cloud,
Winter is waking.

Winter awakes,
Stretching from its sleep of summer,
Like a cat in front of the fire,
Snowing lightly.

Winter grips,
Clutching with its icy grasp,
Like a man with a glass of wine,
Blizzards raging.

Winter tires,
Controlling the blizzards,
Like a battery running out of power,
Winter is dead.

But only to be born next year.

Geraden Wren (11)
Oaklands Primary School, Welwyn

Owl

His eyes are like dark gloomy rooms
His nose is like a stalactite in a cave
His belly is like mist covering hailstones
His fur is as fluffy as a polar bear
His claws are pins.

Emily Tomlinson (9)
Oaklands Primary School, Welwyn

Winter

Winter springs,
Rising over the fiery horizon,
Like a freezing iceberg,
Winter arrives.

The snow glistens,
Falling to the frosty ground,
Like the sinking Titanic
Winter freezes.

The ice sparkles,
Shining on the sparkling moon,
Like the North Pole,
Winter fades.

The coldness creeps,
Tiptoeing closer into the deadly trap,
Like someone's deafening scream,
Winter sets.

Georgina Shortland (10)
Oaklands Primary School, Welwyn

A Polar Bear

His fur is like a fluffy cloud
His ears are snowy mountains
His paws are snowy boots
A nose like a dark black button
Eyes like rubies.

James Curtis (9)
Oaklands Primary School, Welwyn

Cat

His ears are like a snowy mountain,
His claws are as black as wood,   ·
His teeth are vampire's fangs,
His eyes are like torches flickering in the night,
His body is a black and white fur coat.

Katie Genever (8)
Oaklands Primary School, Welwyn

Dog

Ears like the sunset in the sky,
His tail is as long as a snake,
His fur is a dream cloud in the sky,
His legs are short school water bottles,
His ears are two large mountains stuck together.

Vishva Naik (9)
Oaklands Primary School, Welwyn

My Kitten

His whiskers are frozen strings glowing in the darkness,
An ear like a flagpole sticking up,
His paws are razors,
An eye like a marble.

Jamie Kempster (8)
Oaklands Primary School, Welwyn

The Moon

The moon wakes
Ready to stay up all night
Like a brown old owl
Darkness

The moon gazes
Smiles at the bright stars
Like never to be lonely
Midnight

The moon sleeps
Rests so far away
Like drowning pearls
Beautiful giant star.

Rhian Mather (10)
Oaklands Primary School, Welwyn

Fire

Burning fire waves
Gazing all over the grass
Like a frightened creature in the dark

Deadly fire jumps
Blowing all over the grass
Like a rampaging storm at night

Scorching fire creeps
At the dying branches
Like a sneaky and dangerous fox
Left alone.

Joshua Heyman (9)
Oaklands Primary School, Welwyn

Sweets

What I like about chocolate, is the way it melts in your mouth
What I don't like about chocolate, is it makes you thirsty.

What I like about crisps, is they have a nice taste,
What I don't like about crisps, is there's only one flavour I like
Which is prawn cocktail.

What I like about Chewits, is I like chewing them
What I don't like about Chewits, it their silkiness.

What I like about bubblegum, is blowing bubbles,
What I don't like about bubblegum, is the one with no taste.

Mica Wilkins (8)
Purley Oaks Primary School, Croydon

Animals

What I like about animals is the way they move around on the grass
What I dislike about animals is that they sometimes hit you.

What I like about animals is that they are sometimes nice
What I dislike about animals is that they always wander off.

What I like about animals is that they are clever
What I dislike about animals is that they fight a lot.

What I like about animals is that they always know
When they want to do something else
What I dislike about animals is that they don't always listen.

Haiden Noel (8)
Purley Oaks Primary School, Croydon

Space

The sun as our queen and planets as the sun's servants
Space, an empty pitch-black as the children come and light it up
The stars as a disco ball shimmering, a speck of light, lighting up
the disco

The moon is a shining face that makes the world light up
The sun bullying the Earth, following its shoulder
Saturn flying around, bumping into everything.

Manisha Patel (10)
Purley Oaks Primary School, Croydon

Snow

What I like about snow is that I can have fun,
What I hate about snow is that it is freezing down your back.
What I like about snow is you have to wear gloves,
What I hate about snow is that it freezes your ears off.
What I love about the snow is that it is so smooth,
But what I really hate is that it gives you a headache.

Dante Smith (8)
Purley Oaks Primary School, Croydon

Space

Venus, dirty grey and black!
Jupiter, bright colours and also the biggest of them all!
I can see strong rocks spring towards me
I have to try and dodge them
The dark, black night sky, makes me very sleepy.

Samantha Collins (9)
Purley Oaks Primary School, Croydon

Likes And Dislikes

What I hate about chocolate
Is that it's so slimy and fattening
What I like about the PlayStation
Is that it's got connectors
What I hate about rain
Is that it soaks me wet and makes me upset
What I like about my friend
Is how he runs so fast
What I hate about slugs and spiders
Is how they scuttle up my back and they are so slimy
What I like about birthdays
Is that you get lots of cakes
What I hate about snakes
Is they are slithery and creepy.

Nathan Samuel (8)
Purley Oaks Primary School, Croydon

Weather

I like rain because it is soaking wet
I don't like rain because it is wet

I like snow because I love snow fights
I don't like snow because it is freezing cold

I like the sun because I like freezing cold ice cream
I don't like the sun because it gives me sunburn

I like wind because it is breezy
I don't like wind because it makes me cold

I like storms because I like thunder
I don't like storms because they are loud.

Louise Covington (8)
Purley Oaks Primary School, Croydon

Likes And Dislikes

What I like about woodlice
Is that they curl up into balls
What I dislike about woodlice
Is that they are so small
What I like about woodlice
Is that the body is so wrinkly!
What I hate about woodlice
Is that they tickle your hand
What I like about woodlice
Is how they walk
What I hate about woodlice
Is how many legs they have
What I like about woodlice
Is that they have antennas.

Somer Wigger (8)
Purley Oaks Primary School, Croydon

Likes And Dislikes

What I hate about teachers
Is they shout
What I like about teachers
Is they laugh
What I hate about worms
Is when you cut them in half
They turn into another worm
What I like about worms
Is that they are slimy
What I hate about dogs
Is they poo anywhere!
What I like about dogs
Is they are furry.

Mollie Bernadino (8)
Purley Oaks Primary School, Croydon

Likes And Dislikes

What I hate about worms
Is that they are wet and wiggly!
What I like about horses
Is that they let us ride on their backs.
What I hate about slugs
Is that they wiggle about
What I like about cats
Is that they are soft and cuddly.

Perrie Aungmya (8)
Purley Oaks Primary School, Croydon

Space

Darkness!
Lots of planets everywhere
Stars dancing
A black blanket with twinkling lights
The sun, a huge ball of fire
Earth turning in slow motion
Rocks floating
Weightless in space.

Brito Dos Reis (9)
Purley Oaks Primary School, Croydon

Likes And Dislikes

What I hate about toast
Is when you eat one piece, the other piece gets cold
What I like about toast
Is it makes you full up
What I hate about toast
Is when the plate is on the table and the crust is on it
What I like about toast
Is it is really tasty!

Georgina Hilton (7)
Purley Oaks Primary School, Croydon

Likes And Dislikes

What I hate about CBeebies
Is it is for babies
What I hate about rain
Is it always makes me wet
What I like about snow
Is that it is fun to play in
What I like is the sun
Because when it comes out
Everywhere looks lovely!

Haseeb Wajid (7)
Purley Oaks Primary School, Croydon

Space

Stars dancing in space
Asteroids rapidly running by me
Dark holes gushing by me
Sun burning like coal on a barbeque
I saw a Milky bar and it makes me think of the Milky Way
DJ Moony playing his music to the used-up planets
An adult playing frisbee with Uranus
Shevchenko kicking the moon around the Earth.

Jed Moqaddem (9)
Purley Oaks Primary School, Croydon

Space

Never-ending
A river of pitch-black emptiness
Frightfulness
A pathway full of black fear
A sea full of specks of light
Abandoned
A lifeless warehouse full of used-up planets.

Thomas Lockwood (10)
Purley Oaks Primary School, Croydon

Likes And Dislikes

What I hate about spiders
Is they are creepy!
What I like about spiders
Is you can put them down people's back
What I hate about ants
Is they are everywhere
What I like about ants
Is they are strong
What I hate about centipedes
Is that they have one hundred legs
What I like about centipedes
Is they are very long.

Jack Sawyer (8)
Purley Oaks Primary School, Croydon

Likes And Dislikes

What I hate about horses
Is they spend the day getting rid of waste!
What I like about horses
Is they give you bumpy rides
What I hate about horses
Is that they roll over and get themselves muddy!
What I like about horses
Is the way they run, as fast as the wind!
What I hate about horses
Is the way they smell the hay
What I like about horses
Is that they are smooth runners.

Shoamar Best (7)
Purley Oaks Primary School, Croydon

The Windy Day

In the city it was a windy day
A man running from the big black thunder
The wind was punching me all the way back
I was the only one out
Shop doors crashing
It looked like the leaves were chasing me
All the way back
Rain covered the city
Gutters breaking
I thought I was going to die
I could hear the wind
It was going through my ears.

Billy Stracey (10)
Purley Oaks Primary School, Croydon

A Windy Day

Staring outside
I could see the trees
Move!
The gust of wind
Banging like mad
Leaves flying
Like birds in the sky
The wind banging on my classroom door
Like a child knocking on a table
Trees swaying backwards and forwards
Dancing!

Courtney Covington (9)
Purley Oaks Primary School, Croydon

The Sparkling Stars

Stars float across the sky
Stars are made of gas
Stars are big, stars are also small
Stars glisten in the sky
Some people have seen a shooting star
Stars are beautiful and gold
When the stars glisten, they're like bright light bulbs in the sky
Some stars drift away like the clouds
Some stars are as sharp as a knife
Stars are gold, stars are pretty
The stars wink down at us
Stars smile at us
Stars are as pointy as a vampire's teeth
Stars are as shiny as the sun.

Chanel D'Rozario (9)
Purley Oaks Primary School, Croydon

Space

Bottomless!
The enormous sun heats the Milky Way
The planet Jupiter is the prince of space
And the stars are a dancing DJ
John Terry kicking the moon right round the planets
The wide and colossal space is out of this world
Stars, small, bright and shiny
The large black holes gushing by
And meteors crashing down
That is the end of the dark and cold solar system!

Thomas Shepherd (9)
Purley Oaks Primary School, Croydon

Space

In space, the golden stars are floating around
The shooting stars fly and zoom across the sky
Some are big, some are small
The small sparkle
The big are glistening
The moon uses the starlight and sunlight to make it glow
As white as milk is its outside
Other planets are floating around
Mars is blood-red
Neptune is as blue as the sea
Mercury they say is as hot as a sizzling sausage
There is no gravity around
So I drift away into the space's sky.

Zoe Brown (10)
Purley Oaks Primary School, Croydon

Space

Saturn
Mars dirty grey and black
Stars are dancing around in the sky
The Milky Way is a man singing
The sun listens carefully, happy and glad
It is so shiny, it is a man screaming in anger
I can see rocks thumping around
The moon is a woman teaching the stars how to dance
The world is as happy as it ever can be
So night will never end.

Sophie Ward (10)
Purley Oaks Primary School, Croydon

The Shooting Star

I went into space in my flaming hot rocket,
I suddenly saw a star that was near my rocket's socket
It was a star that shot out far
And it went onto Mars
The sun is hot, the Earth is cold, the shooting star is big and bold
It made wishes and ran around
But the bad thing was, it hit the ground
It hurt its head and hurt its arm
But the worst thing is, he burnt his charm
He said, 'Hello,'
He said, 'Goodbye,'
He ran around and played I Spy
The star smiled, the star grinned,
The star went round and pinched the wind
The star is good, the star is bad
The star is round and I am glad.

Sophie Nicholls (9)
Purley Oaks Primary School, Croydon

Space

Peacefully
Godfather blazing and giving the heat
Stars dancing in a powerful, lightning disco
Planets spinning round and round and round
No oxygen, no air, no aliens, no fun
Satellite being on power
Milky Way as tubby as chubby
Stars shoot like a bullet
Kids play football, Mars as the ball
Making me think about the Mars bar.

Hakhilesh Gopaul (10)
Purley Oaks Primary School, Croydon

The Gloomy Autumn Day

I was walking along a gloomy path
And suddenly I saw rain crystals dropping down
I heard thunder
I was scared
Then I felt wind slap my face
I couldn't believe it, the wind was so fierce
I couldn't breathe or stand up
The trees were swaying
The clouds were about to cry
The gutters gurgled, the rain splattered down
A dark swing made a creaking and squeaking noise
The forest called, 'Help me! Help me!'
I could feel the wind blowing my hair
I felt like I was being sucked up by a tornado
I could smell the beef from the café
It was fine
Until
I got hit in the face by flying leaves and paper.

Vikki Billingham (10)
Purley Oaks Primary School, Croydon

The Sun

The sun is the biggest star in space
The sun is as shiny as gold and it is as hot as a volcano
The sun is blazing hot
It always shines when the clouds are gone
The sun moves around the world, day and night
The sun is as orange as carrots
And blinds my eyes when I look at it
The sun blasts in the sky.

Ekow Taylor (11)
Purley Oaks Primary School, Croydon

In Space

The Earth is as big as a balloon and as round as a sphere
The sun is the biggest star in the universe
And the brightest thing in space
The pitch-black sky is as black as an olive
The stars wink down at us
And the moon slowly creeps round the Earth
The planets are nice and round
The planets are multicoloured
The shooting stars whizz down as fast as a cheetah
Mars is as red as blood
Pluto is as small as a pea
And Neptune is as blue as the sea.

Farida Matin (10)
Purley Oaks Primary School, Croydon

The Sun

The sun is as hot as fire burning
Whenever I feel the hotness, I'm always happy
The sun is always blazing hot
It's always happy whenever the clouds are gone
It's always staring at me and it blinds me
The sun is as hot as a volcano
It's as shiny as a piece of gold
The sun is the biggest star I've ever seen
The sun is the happiest star in the universe
The sun is my best friend.

Roy Tandi (10)
Purley Oaks Primary School, Croydon

Space

In outer space
Mars is one of the biggest planets
It is as red as blood
Stars are as gold as a king's crown
The sun is as hot as a volcano
Some stars are big and beautiful
And small and beautiful
Some sparkle, some don't
The moon is as white as snow
And it moves, like a car in a traffic jam
The rocket speeds up in the air
Speeds up in the air
It is as noisy as a digger.

Ryan Martensz (9)
Purley Oaks Primary School, Croydon

Space

The sun is like a blinding light bulb
It doesn't move
It doesn't turn cold
It is as yellow as a banana
As hot as an overburnt radiator
The stars shooting as quickly as a bullet from a gun
They're also nearly as hot as the sun
The moon is as white as the whitest milk
The moon looks like a sheet of paper with holes
A rocket at the speed of lightning
Noisy as a loud herd of elephants.

Connor Koodoruth (10)
Purley Oaks Primary School, Croydon

Space

As my rocket floated in space
Amongst the shooting stars
I saw the moon, as white as milk
Reflecting off the sun
The sun was scalding like a sizzling sausage
I saw Mars as red as blood
The Earth, from space, is like a fragment of sand
I can't see the ozone layer
But I know it is there.

Jonathan Burraway (9)
Purley Oaks Primary School, Croydon

The Rocket

The rocket is as pointy as a sharp knife
As fast as a shooting star
Extremely noisy
And also it is so fast that you can't even see it
Because it is as fast as the wind
Big as a house and hot
Because the rocket drives too much
Floats around space like a lost thing.

Azad Firat (10)
Purley Oaks Primary School, Croydon

Space

Space is a black bag with stars drifting away
Like a baby that is sound asleep
Space is a shooting star
That sparkles in the midnight sky
Space is a face that goes to sleep at midnight.

Jamie Wells (10)
Purley Oaks Primary School, Croydon

The Life In Space

The life in space is good
Because there is no gravity
It is like you can fly
But you know that you can't
When I went to space
I went in a rocket
It was as loud as a herd of elephants
I landed on the moon
And it was as soft as a cloud
I got back into the rocket
And I was going fast
It was like someone was running to the park
But at top speed
I went past Mars
It was a red bloodthirsty planet
And I went past Pluto
It is as small as a pea
From where I could see it.

Adam Collins (10)
Purley Oaks Primary School, Croydon

Space Is Different

Space is different because you can see the planets better
Than looking through a telescope or looking at a map
And on Earth, the sun does not look big
But in outer space, the sun is really big
The sun, I think, is a blazing, on fire meatball
The stars look like they are made of gold
And sparkle so much, you can hardly see them
Saturn is as hot as a sizzling sausage.

Richard Phelps (9)
Purley Oaks Primary School, Croydon

Slaps In The Face

Trees stooping down low like an old man
Leaves dancing one by one in the breeze
Like a slap in the face, the wind hits trees
Do trees have smiley faces?
Tall shadows and small trees
Day and night
Does he get cold or does he not?
Newspapers shuffle by
What a slap in the face he gets!
I smell petrol fumes
And bonfire's smoke
I hear birds, I also see the wavy sea.

Suzy Southall (9)
Purley Oaks Primary School, Croydon

A Journey Into Space

As I flew into space
My favourite things I would have to say
Are the stars
They were gold and beautiful
But most of all
They were as big as houses
As I turned my head around
I saw a shooting star
And I made a wish
My wish was to come back to space
So guess where I am now!

Janique Hutson-Ayim (9)
Purley Oaks Primary School, Croydon

Strange Day

Wind
Whipping the life out of people passing by
The mist
Closing in
Faster . . .
. . . until
The rain splinters the town and shatters the mist
Thunderclaps like a stampede of prehistoric behemoths
A tree is all alone like a person without a face
Lightning
Zaps
Across the gloomy sky
Destroying everything in its path
Suddenly
A change of weather
I see the sun
A leaping fire too hot to go near
The tree enlightens.

Jahan Hussain (10)
Purley Oaks Primary School, Croydon

Space

As I flew into space in the rocket
I could see the stars staring at me
The sun was standing in one position
As I got nearer, I started to realise
That the sun is as hot as a volcano
So I moved away
I saw Mars, that looked as red as blood
And Pluto that was as small as a pea
I turned to the moon, as white as milk
And I landed back on the only civilised planet.

Brandon Murphy (9)
Purley Oaks Primary School, Croydon

The Rogue Elephant

One dark, gloomy afternoon
The trees were blowing
Helplessly with fear
The wind sharply piercing
My stomach so I couldn't
Breathe!
I carried on strolling
But I found it difficult
Because the wind had so much
Power and the force -
It was unbelievable!
Suddenly, the rain pelted down
In rage!
The wind became like
A rogue elephant!
The wind hit me
And it felt like a rogue elephant
Had lifted me up into the air!
I could see its gleaming red eyes!
It had an unusual colour
A misty-grey colour
It felt like it had lifted me up
With its razor-sharp tusks
And suddenly, it flung me up into the air
I fell to the ground
I was in so much pain!
Then suddenly - sun!

Serene Blake (11)
Purley Oaks Primary School, Croydon

The Wind

In the field
There was a
Ghastly tree
Swiftly
The wind blew the leaves
Like it was going to
Blow the
Rusty old
Mysterious tree away
Suddenly
I could hear a funny noise
It was a little girl crying
Suddenly
I had to rub my eyes quickly
Unbelievably
It was a Minotaur
I knew it was a mirage
Or was it not?

Dominic Anning (10)
Purley Oaks Primary School, Croydon

A Windy Day

I can hear the wind growling like a lion
He breaks the gusty trees
The wind punches me in my face
Paper and dust were flying around
The leaves were dancing like a dancer
The door opening and shutting
I could feel that the wind was blowing my ears off
Trees moving like a wolf
The tornado was breaking houses.

Youvraj Sookhraz (10)
Purley Oaks Primary School, Croydon

The Scary Tree

I was walking
In the forest
I could see a big, scary
Gloomy tree
It looked like
A big gorilla
When I looked
At the sky
I could see
Clouds crying
I saw that huge tree
It's bold
I could see his face
It looked scary
Very scary!
I saw one red leaf
Dancing in the air
That tree lost it
Tree
Scary tree.

Dominika Kaminska Murzyniec (9)
Purley Oaks Primary School, Croydon

Space

Moon rotating
A black hole in space
Never stopping
Sun burning
A gigantic volcano
Stars dancing the salsa
Earth, a tiny piece of Blu-tack
Completely silent.

Menkara Maddix (10)
Purley Oaks Primary School, Croydon

The Way I See Space

Stars twirling
Mars hot
They're always awake
Day and night
The sun's
Too bright.

Oh, they're having a disco
Can I come?
All I have to do
Is ask my mum!
They have a BBQ.

All the stars
Gather together
Milky Way is so dreamy and delicious
I wanted to take a bite
Something was superstitious
I felt a shake
It was my mum
I discovered that I was asleep.

Monifah Burke (9)
Purley Oaks Primary School, Croydon

Space

A giant disco ball
Covered in shining stars
UFOs flying in space
A black blanket
Twinkling in the night
A black hole
Sucking up everything
Right out in space.

Zoe Turner (10)
Purley Oaks Primary School, Croydon

Weather

I jogged down the road
Suddenly
The wind belted me
As if I had done something wrong
Suddenly
Hailstones fell as if they were shattered glass
The gust blew me away
The tornado was a barricade wind
I was trapped
Between the tornado and the gust
I ran
But
The gust blew me back
Towards the tornado
Then a raging ball of fire
Burnt the barricade down
And I freed the wind.

Dave Newman (11)
Purley Oaks Primary School, Croydon

The Wind

The dark clouds were stampeding like wildebeest
I felt the wind inject me with its syringe
Nobody was to be seen
I was alone
I saw an ancient tree
Its leaves were like lions' claws
I was so frightened
I never went there again
But one day
The wind started to inject me
Again!

Tony Wu (9)
Purley Oaks Primary School, Croydon

As I Travelled Into Space

The moon is as white as milk
Mars is as red as blood
Pluto is as small as a pea
Saturn is as bright as the sun
Mercury is as hot as a sizzling sausage
Neptune is as blue as the ocean
The sun is shining like gold
The sun is smiling down on me
The rocket is as speedy as a racing car
The stars are glistening like a light bulb
As I floated up to the stars
I started to drift away
The sweet smell of the sizzling sausage
Came floating over to me
The stars winked down on me.

Sian Fisher (10)
Purley Oaks Primary School, Croydon

The Planets And Stars

The Earth is round and the Earth is big
Sometimes it looks like a big fat fig
The sun is scorching, the sun is gold
It sometimes looks like it is bold
Mars is as red as blood
Neptune's as blue as the sea
Pluto looks like an overgrown pea
Mercury is sizzling hot
But the thing is, that Uranus is not
Saturn is bright, Saturn has a ring
But the moon looks like a big white thing
The stars can be big, stars can be small
Some look like a glistening ball.

Dalian Watson (10)
Purley Oaks Primary School, Croydon

My Journey Into Space

The rocket was as pointy as a diamond,
The stars were as massive as a house,
The moon was a milky-white, round ball of fluffy clouds,
The sun was staring up at me with a glistening smile,
Mars was as red as a red-hot chilli pepper,
The Earth looked so pretty with its white top and bottom.
As I got nearer to the sun, I could feel it blazing like a hot volcano,
Speeding past Pluto, I saw it was as small as a pea,
The stars looked like beautiful, drifting gold sparks,
The Earth's ozone layer shone as bright as silver,
In the dazzling moonlight.
As I travelled back to Earth,
The rocket sped away with excitement.

Kym Martin (11)
Purley Oaks Primary School, Croydon

Floating

Floating, drifting, the beautiful stars fly past
I speed past the moon in all its white glory
And the Earth looks so small and pretty
When you look at the top or bottom
Wow!
I was nearly blinded by the sun staring at me
With that great big eye of his
Zoom!
A shooting star blasting by
While I'm way up, past the sky.

Grant Manuel (10)
Purley Oaks Primary School, Croydon

Space

Dark, like non-light night
Odd-shaped stars are all different sizes
And some stars are bright like the sun
Colour is rose-red
Or lemon-yellow
Moon is silver
And it does not stop moving
Earth does not stop too
Its colours are blue, green and white
Space has lots of friends
Sun is always angry
So its colour is blood-red
Space is a kind and enormous person
Because it always puts lots of stars on its body
Space has lots of eyes
And all of that is a different shape
The space is endless!

Haruka Koyama (10)
Purley Oaks Primary School, Croydon

Tornado Day

Alone in my bedroom, sobbing on my bed
I got up and looked out of my window and saw
Clouds forming shapes in the open, spread-out sky
Rain thudding on my window
I could hear a loud bellow of roaring thunder
I could see lightning striking like a cobra
I was about to go and lie down
When I noticed a whirling hurricane heading my way
So I hid under my warm covers on my bed
They felt like the wings of an eagle.

Micaiah Wilkins (10)
Purley Oaks Primary School, Croydon

A Windy Day

Cold like ice
Clouds misty
Clouds crying
And it was thundering
Little birds flying
Wind pushing the birds back
Wind blows so strong
It blows the leaves off the trees
Very, very wet
And damp
Crisp bags flying
Wind blowing waves all over the beach
Wrappers flying like Batman
Clouds, white like milk
Some clouds stop crying
But some clouds keep crying
About to flood the place.

Stefan Greenidge (9)
Purley Oaks Primary School, Croydon

Space

Peaceful
Never-ending
Sharp rocks floating slowly
Stars squish up into a picture
Sun is a king of them all
Colourful Milky Way shoots through the dark hold
Stars dance and twinkle around to a ship
Saturn with a hula-hoop around it
Rocks whizzing around
Space is a galaxy that never ends
A vortex drains everything around it
Sun is a torch that never loses its fire.

Omer Hakki (10)
Purley Oaks Primary School, Croydon

Space

Like space hasn't been alive at all
Stars dancing around
Stars turning into different shapes
An extraordinary sight
Like a frightful dark
Never-ending night
Earth seemed extremely peaceful
Like I've never lived in there before
Rock floating spongely
Bright sun shining, smiling
Powerful as a volcano
Pluto, the darkest planet in the universe
Dressed in black
It was endless
Endless.

Binte Khoyratty (11)
Purley Oaks Primary School, Croydon

Space

Shooting star - like someone running
Galaxy - smooth and sharp rocks moving slowly
Moon - a ball of crescent white
Sun - is the queen of the planets
Earth - a ball of green and blue
Stars - dance while Neptune plays a song
Saturn - likes playing with her hula-hoop
Pluto - a ball of stars lighting up space
Comet - is someone running really fast
Mars - is a lovely chocolate
Neptune - like a field of green and blue
Mercury - whenever the sun calls
Mercury is the first to come.

Zipporah Bannister (9)
Purley Oaks Primary School, Croydon

Space

Looking out of my window
Seeing fireballs moving at five miles an hour!
Everything was pitch-black
There were stars dancing
It was so magical
I tried to look at the sun, but she was too bright
I saw the Milky Way and it looked so delicious
I saw Mars and it made me think of a nice Mars bar
I really couldn't believe my eyes
Seeing all these things made me think of a disco
People always say to me, stop staring out at space
But now I really am
I saw a black hole, twirling which gave me a fright
That made me want to go home
So off to Earth I went.

Carlisa Kyte (10)
Purley Oaks Primary School, Croydon

Space

I saw stars blinking at me like glitter
I saw asteroids whizzing towards me with deadly flames
I had to dodge them
I saw Saturn, I decided to see who can do the best tricks
With his hula-hoop, but unfortunately Saturn won
I was astonished when I saw the Milky Way
When I hear that word, I think of milk
Then I noticed it was like a bunch of colourful stars
Squashed together, spinning all the time
I saw stars driving around, into the shape of a racing car
I kept on thinking, it was me driving.

Stephon Best (9)
Purley Oaks Primary School, Croydon

Like And Hate

What I like about football
Is that I get stronger at doing amazing goals
What I hate about being a goalie
Is that when I miss the ball, I get in terrible trouble
With the other players
What I like about passing the ball
Is that then I don't have to run extremely long after the ball
What I really hate about football
Is that sometimes I get mud all over me
What I like about football
Is that the rules are very fair
What I really hate about football
Is that the other team always want to make me fail!

Samuel Conan (8)
Purley Oaks Primary School, Croydon

Love And Hate

What I hate about apples
Is they are really terrible and they hurt my gums
What I love about apples
Is they are very, very gorgeous
What I hate about oranges
Is they are horrible when the juice gets in your eyes, it really hurts
What I love about oranges
Is the sweetness
What I hate about melon
Is when the juice comes out, it drips and it's sticky
What I really, really like about melons
Is the colour and the soft bit at first.

K-ci Ladega (8)
Purley Oaks Primary School, Croydon

Like And Hate

What I like about lollipops
Is they're sugary
What I hate about lollipops
Is they're sticky
What I like about lollipops
Is they're juicy
What I hate about lollipops
Is they give you holes in your teeth
What I like about lollipops
Is they're sour
What I hate about lollipops
Is they come in green
What I like about lollipops
Is they're yummy
What I hate about lollipops
Is they're small
What I like about lollipops
Is they're different colours
What I really, really like about lollipops
Is you can get big, fat ones
What I really, really hate about lollipops
They get really wet.

Tyler Jade John (7)
Purley Oaks Primary School, Croydon

Out Of This World

Empty
Heartless and cold
Quiet and silent
Milky Way like a toddler let loose with paint
Rocks gently float past
Stars glow on their own light
Out of this world
Night
Endless night.

Luke Callaway (10)
Purley Oaks Primary School, Croydon

Space

Amazing
Rocks running by
The gigantic shiny white teeth
Floating by
Eight colourful planets
Left behind
The burning sun
The orangey Mars
The sea-blue and grass-green Earth
And the milky-white moon
Look out!
The dreadful asteroid
Coming nearer and nearer
Sadly, I can't see this every day.

Farid Rahman (10)
Purley Oaks Primary School, Croydon

A Windy Day

In the street, cars passing by
The sky thunders like lions *roaring!*
Newspapers flying like birds
I can hear *thunder!*
Drawing pictures
In the
Sky
I can see trees losing their leaves
Like people losing their blood
Rain pushing
People to the ground
The wind blowing left and right
People shivering day and night.

Michael Appiah (10)
Purley Oaks Primary School, Croydon

Love And Hate

What I love about maths
Is it is good for us
What I hate about maths
Is I get it wrong sometimes
What I love about the playground
Is because it's big
What I hate about the playground
Is because we are not allowed to race
What I love about the gym
Is we do PE in it
What I hate about the gym
Is you can get hurt
What I love about PE
Is we do football skills
What I hate about PE
Is I cut myself once
What I love about the singing room
Is I love to sing
What I hate about the singing room
Is I get the words wrong.

Mason Baum-Shaw (9)
Purley Oaks Primary School, Croydon

Love And Hate

What I hate about school
Is that my friend hates me
What I like about school
Is that I'm doing my work
What I hate about school
Is that there's no one else to play with me
Because no one likes me
What I like about school
Is spelling and I know my five times table.

Veemala Calleechurrun (8)
Purley Oaks Primary School, Croydon

Love And Hate

What I love about puppies
Is their great, silky skin
What I hate about puppies
Is that when they come in, they leave a trail of footprints
What I love about cats
Is when they purr with happiness
What I hate about cats
Is they leave hair everywhere
What I love about dogs
Is their extremely soft fur on their backs
What I hate about dogs
Is when they bite you
What I really, really love about lions
Is their humungous manes
What I really, really hate about lions
Is that they roar loudly.

Alex Milson (8)
Purley Oaks Primary School, Croydon

Love And Hate

What I hate about mangos
Is they are squishy and slimy
What I love about mangos
Is they're big and take a long time to finish
What I hate about mangos
Is they're always the same
What I love about mangos
Is the weird and amazing smell of them
What I hate about mangos
Is they're a bit big
What I love about mangos
Is they are green and yellow
What I hate about mangos is simple
I have to wait till they're ripe.

Liam Simmonds (8)
Purley Oaks Primary School, Croydon

Love And Hate

What I hate about football
Is you get dirty and extremely hot
What I love about football
Is you can be as noisy as possible
What I hate about football
Is you get whiffy
What I love about football
Is that you can run super fast
What I hate about football
Is that you fall over and damage yourself
What I love about football
Is that it's good exercise
What I really hate about football
Is that when you are in goal, the ball is always shooting.

Lacey Booth (8)
Purley Oaks Primary School, Croydon

Like And Hate

What I like about playtime
Is that you get to play
What I hate about playtime
Is that we only get 15 minutes
What I like about PE
Is that we get exercise
What I hate about PE
Is that you can hurt yourself
What I like about the gym
Is that it's big
What I hate about the gym
Is that it smells.

Sharic Morton-Johnson (8)
Purley Oaks Primary School, Croydon

Likes And Dislikes

What I like about butterflies
Is they have beautiful colours on them
What I hate about worms
Is they are slimy
What I like about snails
Is they crunch when you stamp on them
What I like about my mummy
Is she gives me cuddles
What I hate about my sister
Is that she bites me and my mummy
What I like about my dad
Is that he takes me out
What I hate about spiders
Is they have hairy legs
What I like about roller skates
Is that they make you go fast
What I hate about head lice
Is that they make you itch.

Loreena May Fonceca-Butler (7)
Purley Oaks Primary School, Croydon

Love And Hate

What I love about tennis
Is that it is a fantastic sport
What I hate about football
Is it is so terrible for me
What I love about food
Is it can make me fit
What I hate about food
Is it can make you fat.

Rose Agalliu (8)
Purley Oaks Primary School, Croydon

Love And Hate

What I hate about my dress
Is that it is skinny
What I love about my dress
Is that it is beautiful
What I hate about my top
Is that it shrank in the washing machine
What I love about my top
Is that it is snazzy
What I hate about my shorts
Is that they are short
What I love about my shorts
Is that they are nice
And what I really hate about my jeans
Is that they're tiny.

Nwamaka Agbandje (7)
Purley Oaks Primary School, Croydon

Love And Hate

What I hate about cats
Is when they leave disgusting footprints all over the clean floor
What I love about cats
Is their soft fur coats
What I hate about cats
Is when they try to scratch you with their sharp claws which is hurtful
What I love about cats
Is when they purr beautifully with happiness
What I hate about cats
Is when they leave their hair on your bed, which is annoying
What I really love about cat
Is when they eat their smelly food.

Courtney O'Reilly (8)
Purley Oaks Primary School, Croydon

Like And Hate

What I like about clothes
Is that they are really warm
What I hate about clothes
Is they can sometimes be itchy and that is terrible
What I like about clothes
Is you can get them really, really dirty
What I hate about clothes
Is they hurt you really badly
What I like about clothes
Is that they're really soft
What I hate about clothes
Is they badly scratch you
What I really, really like about clothes
Is they are really warm and snugly
What I really, really hate about clothes
Is the girly clothes are not my type at all.

Olivia Woolacott (7)
Purley Oaks Primary School, Croydon

Love And Hate

What I hate about wrestling
Is that when they are going to hit them with a chair
It absolutely stops for a bit
What I love about wrestling
Is the wicked players like John Cena
What I hate about wrestling
Is the rubbish adverts in the middle of it
What I love about wrestling
Is the wicked toys and arena you can buy in the shops
What I hate about wrestling
Is when you buy them in shops they are not cheap.

Jack Theobald (8)
Purley Oaks Primary School, Croydon

Weather

I like rain because I like getting wet
I hate rain because I hate having wet play in school
I like snow because I like having snowball fights
I hate snow because I hate someone throwing a large ball at me
I like sun because the colour is really nice
I hate sun because of the heat
I like cloudy days because the curly-swirly curls around it
I hate cloudy days because it is a boring weather
There is no whipping or whooping
I like windy days because it whooshes and it whoops
I hate windy days because wherever I go, it blows me everywhere
I like misty days because when you're in the car no one can see you
I hate misty days because you can't see anything.

Monica Patel (8)
Purley Oaks Primary School, Croydon

Likes And Dislikes

I hate coyotes
Because they are scary, dangerous and fierce
I like horses
Because they are cute, big, smooth and gentle
I hate turtles
Because they are hard, heavy and they hide from you
I like spiders
Because they spin nice webs and have eight legs
I like dogs
Because they are cute, little and adorable
I hate ants
Because they are tiny and they are everywhere.

Joshua Shepherd (7)
Purley Oaks Primary School, Croydon

Pets

I like my goldfish
Because they play chase
I hate my goldfish
Because they eat the food then spit it out
I like my cat
Because she purrs when I stroke her
I hate my cat
Because she lays on top of me in bed
I like my dog
Because I throw the ball over the washing line
And she jumps up to catch it
I hate my dog
Because she barks really loud
I like my hamster
Because of the way it hops on the wheel
And spins around very, very fast
I hate my hamster
Because it throws the sawdust
I like my snake
Because I like the feel of it
Slithering slowly in my hands
I hate my snake
Because it eats frozen mice
And it makes me feel sick.

Claire Fowler (8)
Purley Oaks Primary School, Croydon

Fruit

I love bananas because they are so smooth
I hate apples because they are very hard
I like passion fruit because they are bright colours
I hate blueberries because I don't like blueberry pie
I love oranges because they are so, so, so juicy
I hate pears because they have no flavour
I love grapes because they taste great.

Hayley Wells (7)
Purley Oaks Primary School, Croydon

The Journey

Ten! The rocket is about to bolt into
The pitch-black place we call space.

Nine! When the engines start blasting
It sounds like a volcano erupting.

Eight! Blazing, blasting, the rocket groans
As it goes adventuring to that bleak place.

Seven! Squeaking like a mouse
The metal's keeping it together.

Six! We grow closer
Our heads hurt.

Five! The metal bar of the flag
Is making my hand sweat.

Four! Downward goes
What is left of our shuttle.

Three! Out we walk
Onto the sand as white as milk.

Two! We stab the pole
Into the ground.

One! *Blast-off!*

Sharoze Faisal (9)
Purley Oaks Primary School, Croydon

Likes And Dislikes

What I like about pizza
Is the taste
What I hate about girls
Is they annoy me in class
What I like about school
Is PE
What I hate about coyotes
Is they eat flesh.

Charlie Warner (8)
Purley Oaks Primary School, Croydon

Weather

What I like about the sun
Is how it warms you up
What I don't like about the sun
Is you get sunburnt
What I like about snow
Is you get to play snowball fights
What I don't like about snow
Is you can't go shopping
What I like about wind
Is it cools you down
What I don't like about wind
Is it blows your hat off
What I like about hail
Is the sound of it tapping on your window
What I don't like about hail
Is when it taps on your head
What I like about rain
Is you get to jump in puddles
What I don't like about rain
Is you can't play outside.

Ashley Southall (8)
Purley Oaks Primary School, Croydon

Likes And Dislikes

What I hate about slugs
Is that they are slimy and creepy
What I like about slugs
Is that they are good for the soil
What I hate about slugs
Is that they get caught in spiders' webs
What I like about slugs
Is because they leave an intricate trail.

Pavithran Srikumaran (9)
Purley Oaks Primary School, Croydon

Likes And Dislikes

What I like about dogs
Is that they have lovely voices and are pretty
What I hate about dogs
Is that they bark at me
What I like about birds
Is that they are pretty and lovely
What I hate about birds
Is that they are noisy
What I like about cats
Is when they are asleep, they are pretty
What I hate about cats
Is sometimes they are noisy and dirty
What I like about monkeys
Is that they can climb a tree
What I hate about monkeys
Is that sometimes they are noisy.

Hinano Koyama (8)
Purley Oaks Primary School, Croydon

Like And Hate

What I hate about basketball
Is when you shoot and you miss
You think it is a terrible shot
What I like about basketball
Is when no one is looking
You can do a fantastic, fabulous pass to another player
What I hate about basketball
Is when someone scares you by bumping into you
What I like about basketball
Is when no one is looking
And you can do some tremendous skill on people.

Requon Lunt (8)
Purley Oaks Primary School, Croydon

Likes And Dislikes

What I like about dogs
Is that they are furry and make me want to cuddle them
What I hate about cheese
Is it tastes disgusting
What I like about crisps
Is they taste so crispy, they make me want to eat ten bags
What I hate about colds
Is the taste running down my throat, it is so disgusting!

Christopher Haraszti (8)
Purley Oaks Primary School, Croydon

Love And Hate

What I love about football
Is that you can do fabulous skills
What I hate about football
Is the terrible referees
What I love about swimming
Is that you can sneak underwater
What I hate about swimming
Is you can drown underwater.

Keenan Morrison (9)
Purley Oaks Primary School, Croydon

Space

Firebombs are a man bursting out of a box
The stars dance on top of the moonlight
Gigantic rocks spinning round and round on the Earth
The sun is playing football with a little toddler
The Milky Way reminds me of eating a Milky Way bar
Mars is a round tomato melting in my mouth.

Jessica May Ledger (9)
Purley Oaks Primary School, Croydon

Pets Poem

What I like about cats
Is they are cute
What I dislike about cats
Is they are dirty
What I like about dogs
Is they guard us safely
What I dislike about dogs
Is they bite us roughly
What I like about hamsters
Is they are small
What I dislike about hamsters
Is they run away quickly
What I like about snakes
Is they don't sleep
What I dislike about snakes
Is they are poisonous
What I like about chameleons
Is they change their colour nicely
What I dislike about chameleons
Is they eat insects badly
What I like about guinea pigs
Is their hair is very soft
What I dislike about guinea pigs
Is they eat smelly food.

Anish Parchure (9)
Purley Oaks Primary School, Croydon

Space

Never-ending
The sun is the king of them all
The sun is the middle of the dark, mysterious dancing ring
Saturn is a giant frisbee with a gigantic ball
A shooting star is a rocket about to launch
Stars dancing around Saturn's huge skating rink.

Giani Ashley (10)
Purley Oaks Primary School, Croydon

Weather

What I like about the sun
Is you get to play in beautiful weather
What I dislike about the sun
Is it gets boiling hot
What I like about the rain
Is you get soaking wet
What I dislike about rain
Is you don't get to play in beautiful weather
What I like about the wind
Is it cools you down
What I dislike about the wind
Is it blows your hat off
What I like about hail
Is it smashes on your windows
What I dislike about hail
Is it quickly hits your head
What I like about snow
Is you get to make huge snowmen
What I dislike about snow
Is it's freezing cold
What I like about twisters
Is they look cool
What I dislike about twisters
Is they destroy houses.

Dharumvir Maharaj (8)
Purley Oaks Primary School, Croydon

Space

Saturn hula-hooping into a competition
While Uranus let off a deadly gas
The universe is a man's organs
The Milky Way, creamy like Turkish delight
Blue sea Neptune
While the stars are mini disco balls.

Brandon Aung-Mya (10)
Purley Oaks Primary School, Croydon

Likes And Dislikes

What I hate about spiders
Is that they are hairy
What I like about rain
Is that it is wet
What I hate about my sister
Is she is annoying
What I like about my mum
Is she is kind and lovely
What I hate about my dad
Is he's grumpy
What I like about my dad
Is he's happy.

Kyra Lord-Lindsay (7)
Purley Oaks Primary School, Croydon

Likes And Dislikes

What I like about snakes
Is they are slimy and slithery
What I dislike about some teachers
Is they shout at me
What I like about myself
Is that they creep up on you
What I dislike about my cousin Chantelle
Is that she annoys me but I still love her
As she is my family!

Sherelle Greenidge-Ifill (7)
Purley Oaks Primary School, Croydon

Likes And Hates

What I hate about slugs
Is they're big and slimy
What I like about wolf dogs
Is that they're scary
What I hate about butterflies
Is that they're pretty
What I like about vultures
Is they're huge and have sharp claws
What I hate about my cousin
Is that he is very rude
What I like about spiders
Is that they're huge and scary.

James Lockwood (7)
Purley Oaks Primary School, Croydon

Likes And Dislikes

I don't like bats
Because I have two bats called Snow and Rainbow
I don't like spiders
Because I don't like their black legs
I like dogs
Because I have a dog called Bam-Bam
I like cats
Because I have a cat called Rose
I don't like rats
Because they have teeth
I like giving horses apples.

Tamikaine Trimblett (8)
Purley Oaks Primary School, Croydon

How I Saw The Planets

I went on a rocket
It was very scary
Then I looked out of the window
And I saw Mars
It was as red as blood
Mars raged a red colour.

I went a mile and saw a star
As glistening as a golden chain
It was as pointy as a knife.

I sat down for an hour
And saw Mercury
I felt as hot as a sizzling sausage.

After a while
I got blinded by Saturn
Because it was as bright as the sun.

Soon I came to Pluto
It was as small as a pea
And a similar colour to an oak tree.

Then I came to Neptune
It was as blue as the sky
But not as long.

Finally, I came to a stop
I got to the moon
It smiled at me.

Cira Fisher-Jaine (9)
Purley Oaks Primary School, Croydon

Books

I like books
Because they're spooky
I hate books
When you don't understand a word or sentence
I like books
Because of the fact they have about 100 pages in them
I hate books
When they start a new line when they've not finished a word
I like books
Because they're funny
I hate books
Because they're sometimes too big
I like books
Because they've got a good front cover
I hate books
Because they're heavy
I like books
Because they set the numbers out nicely
I hate books
Because they can't fit into your bag
I like books
Because they take a short amount of time to read
I hate books
Because you're not allowed to colour in on them.

Harvey Norman (8)
Purley Oaks Primary School, Croydon

All My Thoughts On Books

What I like about books is they are interesting
What I don't like about books is they can be easy
What I like about books is they are long
What I don't like about books is they can be scary
What I like about books is they are fantastic
What I don't like about books is they are not very funny.

Yasmin Basith (7)
Purley Oaks Primary School, Croydon

Animals

What I like about dogs is their fur
What I hate about dogs is their teeth
What I like about cats is their eyes
What I hate about cats is their teeth
What I like about rabbits is their tails
What I hate about rabbits is their claws
What I like about fish is their mouths
What I hate about fish is their scales
What I like about sharks are their noses
What I hate about sharks is their teeth.

Daniel Allen (7)
Purley Oaks Primary School, Croydon

Likes And Dislikes

I hate chips because they're too greasy
I like chips because they're yummy
I hate slugs because they're too slimy
I like slugs because they're fun to play with
I hate the sun because it makes me sweat
I like the sun because I can play in my garden
I hate the snow because it is cold
I like the snow because you can throw snowballs
I hate school because I hate maths
I like school because I can play with my friends.

Morgan Payne (8)
Purley Oaks Primary School, Croydon

The Slithering Snake

The slithering snake
Slithers through the grass
You would be lucky if she let you pass
For she wants her own space
And no one to take her place

She is as fast as lightning
And can be very frightening
But slides as graceful as a feather
And does not care whatever the weather

She's a serpent, scaly and smooth
Who definitely knows how to move
She is a very squidgy reptile
My favourite slithering snake by a mile!

Grace Victoria Perryman (8)
St John's CE (VA) Primary School, Clifton

Sea Sadness

Standing in the sea
Looking down at the water
Watching fish go by
Wanting to be there in the middle of it all
But stuck up here all alone
No friend
No fish
No mum
Not even a lobster to talk to.

Robert Winslow (8)
St John's CE (VA) Primary School, Clifton

Slithery Snakes

Slithery snakes, scaly snakes,
Moving really fast.
Slimy as a snail,
Slithering right past.

Slithery snakes, scaly snakes,
Just as fast as lightning.
When you see one coming by,
It is very frightening.

Slithery snakes, scaly snakes,
Scary when they hiss.
Has a tongue like a fork,
It's a noise you cannot miss.

Slithery snakes, scaly snakes,
Its body like a coil,
Sticks to you like sticky tape,
Then slides into the soil.

Holly Tasker (8)
St John's CE (VA) Primary School, Clifton

Slithery Snakes

Silent snakes stir in the early morning,
While rattlesnakes give a warning
So scary, so loud, just while the sun in dawning.

They slither so slowly, then suddenly attack,
The poor, helpless victim now only sees black,
Poisoned fangs sink deeper and deeper into its back.

The diamondback swallows the fat rat whole,
He is very pleased; he has reached his goal,
He can now return to his camouflaged hole.

Leo Stross (8)
St John's CE (VA) Primary School, Clifton

The Garden

Sitting in the garden
Looking at flowers
And watching next door play
I'm wanting to be there
Playing that good game
But stuck in this growing garden
No friend
No family
Not even an ant to talk to.

Charlotte Jones (8)
St John's CE (VA) Primary School, Clifton

I Love My Rabbits

I have two rabbits that live in a cage
Snowy is white and Dusty is grey
I feed them fresh hay every single day
Which makes them run about and play
I clean them out every Sunday
But the cage is always messy by Monday!
I love my rabbits!

Bethany Tottles (8)
St John's CE (VA) Primary School, Clifton

The Nasty Spider

There was a nasty spider
The big beast
Lives in the soil
It looks hairy
And scary
It's as fat as a hog
Looks like a frog
And smells like a dog.

George Price Hulin (8)
St John's CE (VA) Primary School, Clifton

Sitting In The Street

Sitting in the street
Begging for money
Watching children play
Seeing lovely people
Crying out loud
Crying my eyes out
Only have 50p
Waiting for more
Watching cars go by
Sitting down all the time
No mum
No dad
No sister
No brother
No cat
No dog
Not even a spider to talk to.

James Owens (8)
St John's CE (VA) Primary School, Clifton

Dreadful Desert

Stood in the desert
Looking all around
Staring at the cacti
Growing from the ground
Looking at a scorpion
Hunting for food
And the deadly spiders
In their bad mood
There's no people
No camels
Not even a snake to talk to.

Oliver Beaumont (7)
St John's CE (VA) Primary School, Clifton

Cricket

Sitting on the
Bench
Waiting to be
Picked
I went on
And hit a
Six
So close to
Being caught
But it went
In a tennis
Court
Got a four
By hitting it
On the floor
I was not
Bowled out
Without a doubt.

Adam Shaw (8)
St John's CE (VA) Primary School, Clifton

Harvest Joy

We eat corn
We buy seeds
Thank you God
For your good deeds
We need grain
To grow corn
So let's celebrate
In a harvest festival!

Harry Wood (8)
St John's CE (VA) Primary School, Clifton

Sad On The Seaside

Sitting on the
Seaside
Glancing at
The sea
Watching folks
Charge past
Wishing I
Were playing
With someone
But here I am
All alone
No friends
No brother
No sister
Not even a fish
To talk to.

Jake Guest (8)
St John's CE (VA) Primary School, Clifton

Eight-Legged Freaks

Spiders are scary
They are hairy
They are creepy
They are very
Leapy and sleepy
They make some
Weepy
Because
They are creepy
But I don't think
They are scary
Because
They are hairy!

Jack Ellis (8)
St John's CE (VA) Primary School, Clifton

The Happy Horse

Gentle horse munching on some grass
She has got grass stains on her back
She runs off to see her friends, they call out to each other
Lovely, gentle and happy horse

Her coat is as black as night
It feels very soft, like a teddy
She is sheltering under trees
Lovely, gentle and happy horse

Her name is Heather
And now she has relaxed and gone to sleep
She was very tired
Lovely, gentle and happy horse.

Alexandra Gledhill (8)
St John's CE (VA) Primary School, Clifton

My Cat

My cat is a growler,
My cat is a prowler,
My cat can't catch mice,
She doesn't think they're very nice.

My cat sleeps on the floor,
My cat sleeps near the door,
My cat sleeps on my bed,
My cat pretends to be dead.

My cat is very lazy,
My cat drives me crazy,
My cat lays on my knee,
My cat loves me.

Anya Finch (8)
St John's CE (VA) Primary School, Clifton

Scaly Snakes

Scaly snakes slide along the ground
Scaly snakes make not a sound
Delicate as a flower it slides down
On its way, it makes a frown
Slippery as ice, it goes down a slide
Graceful as a goose, it goes on its side
Strong as a sea lion, it springs one down
On its way, it goes through a town
Speedy as a scorpion, it slithers over one
On its way, it eats a ton
It eats people over thirty-two
It's on its way to get you!

Daniel Newton (8)
St John's CE (VA) Primary School, Clifton

Scaly Whale

Squirting water like her mother taught her
She travels for miles
And never seems to smile
Squirting water from above
She gives a lot of love
She rides the waves
And the other fish are amazed
At her size and strength
And enormous length
Moving in slow motion
Like the queen of the ocean.

Emily Rebecca Hirst (8)
St John's CE (VA) Primary School, Clifton

The Unknown Creature

The beast is ready to pounce
All eight eyes are staring at me
Its fangs are deadly
It's a hairy thing
It's coming towards me, oh no . . .

It's massive! It's as deadly as a devil
As black as the night sky
Its big, fearsome body is like a bulldozer
Barging its way through the dirt
But it's only a little spider
What am I scared of?

Dominic Heyhoe (8)
St John's CE (VA) Primary School, Clifton

Flutter-by Butterfly

Flutter-by butterfly
Fly away
Flutter-by butterfly
See you the next day
Flutter-by butterfly
How graceful you do fly
Flutter-by butterfly
Because of your wings
It makes me flutter-by
Butterfly wings.

Charlotte Anne Tankard (8)
St John's CE (VA) Primary School, Clifton

Sarah's Horse Count

The horse I see is big
The horse I see is friendly
Is it because I give him Polo mints?

The horse I see is brown
The horse I see is smooth
His hair is soft and silky
And makes him shine.

The horse I see is not fat
The horse I see has slim legs
He is a race horse!

Andrew Owen (8)
St John's CE (VA) Primary School, Clifton

Lonely Football Player

Sitting on the bench
Waiting to go on
Looking at the floor
Watching their shadows
Go around wanting to
Run around on the pitch
Be stuck on the bench
No manager
No teammate
No friend
Not even an orange bib to talk to.

Callum Wilkie (8)
St John's CE (VA) Primary School, Clifton

Goodbye Spider

It started in the kitchen
Crawling up the wall
There it was
Ten feet tall
A hairy black spider
With its fierce fangs
Jumped on the cutlery
And made a loud bang

It ran across the worktop
And stopped to have a look
There it was
Reading a book
It was feeling very thirsty
So it swung over to the sink
And with its spiky feelers
It stopped to have a drink

It was over by the window
Creeping along the floor
There it was
Running for the door
It could see into the garden
Where it was sunny and dry
So with its black hairy legs
It waved goodbye.

Siân Lewis (8)
St John's CE (VA) Primary School, Clifton

Spider's Like

As black as the night sky
As furry as a monkey
As fast as a racing car
As scary as a lion.

Joshua Maskill (8)
St John's CE (VA) Primary School, Clifton

Evacuation

Being lonely and feeling sad
Leaving behind your mum and dad.
Seeing fields with long green grass
Cows and sheep gathered in a herd
Get on the train, steaming away
Feeling like you will never see your mum and dad again
Being chosen from the village hall
Going somewhere you don't know at all
Back on the train going home
Evacuees being in the city
A bit messy indeed
But it's my home, where I want to be
A hug from me to my mum and dad
I'm happy to be where I am
My mum, my dad and me care that you can see
My mum, my dad and me.

Tiegan Hezzell (8)
Two Moors Primary School, Tiverton

I See A Cat

He rubs his head against you gently
He wiggles his bottom when he walks
And when he's getting ready to pounce
Black like night, white, the same as a soft cloud
And grey like the sky when it rains
Fluffy like a fluff ball
Silky, the same as a blanket
Miaows loud like a bomb
Sleeps on and on like a lazy sleeping bag
Fights with the other cats badly.

Kayleigh Messenger (8)
Two Moors Primary School, Tiverton

I See A Guinea Pig

I see a guinea pig
Grazing in its run
Running through the breeze
Black as ebony and white as a cloud
Long, like a sausage dog
Smooth as my jumper
Squeak, squeak
There it goes again.

Charlotte Chidgey (8)
Two Moors Primary School, Tiverton

I See A Dog

I see a dog
Running around the house
Black and white, like stars shining at night
Shaped as a cheetah
Rough as a carpet
Makes a bark like a pelican
Charges and bites at people
And sniffles when it cries.

Kayleigh Harris (8)
Two Moors Primary School, Tiverton

September The 1st, 1939

Crying at breakfast
Washing in a bowl of water
Weeping on the train
With my gas mask
Sitting in a padded seat.

Matthew Hunt (8)
Two Moors Primary School, Tiverton

Shark

I see a shark
Ready to strike her prey
Swishing its tail from left to right
Dark blue as the night sky
Shaped, with spiked fins
Rough as concrete
Slamming its teeth together
Breathes from her gills
Then suddenly she strikes.

Alfie Hay (8)
Two Moors Primary School, Tiverton

Shark

I see a shark,
Striking its prey,
While moving fast and right,
White and blue skin,
Shaped like a large plump balloon,
Rough like sandpaper,
Bubbles when it moves,
Breathes from its gills,
Suddenly, it retreats.

James Saunders (8)
Two Moors Primary School, Tiverton

Evacuee

Children crying
Mum leaving
Friends cheering
Getting chosen
I'm the last one there
Slurping my cup of tea.

Bayley Howard (8)
Two Moors Primary School, Tiverton

Evacuation

Kids crying
Mums waving
Getting on the train
Waving bye
Setting off
To find a new home
Seeing fields rush by
The station draws near
The train stops
Everyone gets off
Time to find a new home.

Max Warner-Housego (8)
Two Moors Primary School, Tiverton

Animal

I see a king cobra
Pouncing up a tree
Slithering and jumping
Blended with the tree trunk
Thin and as big as a pencil
Skin all slimy and sticky
Hisses for food
Attacks anything in sight
The most dangerous snake in the world.

Ethan Jones (8)
Two Moors Primary School, Tiverton

September The 1st, 1939

Getting off the puffing train
Hearing the door opening
Listening to the other evacuees
Whispering
Hearing the train's puff
With my mum and dad
Shivering like a spring
The people grinning at me
I thought I did something wrong.

Hema Mistry (8)
Two Moors Primary School, Tiverton

My Exciting Journey

Squeaky track creaking
Mum and Dad weeping
Into a crowd I go
Toot, toot goes the whistle
Off we go into a cloud of smoke
Missing Mum already
Off the train at number nine
Squeaky gate opening.

Shannon Willis (8)
Two Moors Primary School, Tiverton

Young Writers Information

We hope you have enjoyed reading this book - and that you will continue to enjoy it in the coming years.

If you like reading and writing poetry drop us a line, or give us a call, and we'll send you a free information pack.

Alternatively if you would like to order further copies of this book or any of our other titles, then please give us a call or log onto our website at www.youngwriters.co.uk

**Young Writers Information
Remus House
Coltsfoot Drive
Peterborough
PE2 9JX**

(01733) 890066